Amazon GuardDuty Amazon Guard Duty User Guide

A catalogue record for this book is available from the Hong Kong Public Libraries.

Published in Hong Kong by Samurai Media Limited.

Email: info@samuraimedia.org

ISBN 9789888408856

Contents

What Is Amazon GuardDuty?

Amazon GuardDuty is a continuous security monitoring service that analyzes and processes the following data sources: VPC Flow Logs, AWS CloudTrail event logs, and DNS logs. It uses threat intelligence feeds, such as lists of malicious IPs and domains, and machine learning to identify unexpected and potentially unauthorized and malicious activity within your AWS environment. This can include issues like escalations of privileges, uses of exposed credentials, or communication with malicious IPs, URLs, or domains. For example, GuardDuty can detect compromised EC2 instances serving malware or mining bitcoin. It also monitors AWS account access behavior for signs of compromise, such as unauthorized infrastructure deployments, like instances deployed in a region that has never been used, or unusual API calls, like a password policy change to reduce password strength.

GuardDuty informs you of the status of your AWS environment by producing security findings that you can view in the GuardDuty console or through Amazon CloudWatch events.

Pricing for GuardDuty

For information about GuardDuty pricing, see Amazon GuardDuty Pricing.

Accessing GuardDuty

You can work with GuardDuty in any of the following ways:

GuardDuty Console
https://console.aws.amazon.com/guardduty
The console is a browser-based interface to access and use GuardDuty.

AWS SDKs
AWS provides software development kits (SDKs) that consist of libraries and sample code for various programming languages and platforms (Java, Python, Ruby, .NET, iOS, Android, and more). The SDKs provide a convenient way to create programmatic access to GuardDuty. For information about the AWS SDKs, including how to download and install them, see Tools for Amazon Web Services.

GuardDuty HTTPS API
You can access GuardDuty and AWS programmatically by using the GuardDuty HTTPS API, which lets you issue HTTPS requests directly to the service. For more information, see the Amazon GuardDuty API Reference.

How Amazon GuardDuty Uses Its Data Sources

To detect unauthorized and unexpected activity in your AWS environment, GuardDuty analyzes and processes data from AWS CloudTrail event logs, VPC Flow Logs, and DNS logs. The logs from these data sources are stored in the Amazon S3 buckets. GuardDuty accesses them there using the HTTPS protocol. While in transit from these data sources to GuardDuty, all of the log data is encrypted. GuardDuty extracts various fields from these logs for profiling and anomaly detection, and then discards the logs.

The following sections describe the details of how GuardDuty uses each supported data source.

Topics

- AWS CloudTrail event logs
- VPC Flow Logs
- DNS logs

AWS CloudTrail event logs

AWS CloudTrail provides you with a history of AWS API calls for your account, including API calls made using the AWS Management Console, the AWS SDKs, the command line tools, and higher-level AWS services. CloudTrail also allows you to identify which users and accounts called AWS APIs for services that support CloudTrail, the source IP address that the calls were made from, and when the calls occurred. For more information, see What is AWS CloudTrail?

You can configure CloudTrail trails to log management events and/or data events. Management events provide insight into management operations that are performed on resources in your AWS account. For example, configuring security (IAM AttachRolePolicy API operations), registering devices (Amazon EC2 CreateDefaultVpc API operations), configuring rules for routing data (Amazon EC2 CreateSubnet API operations), or setting up logging (AWS CloudTrail CreateTrail API operations). Data events provide insight into the resource operations performed on or within a resource. For example, Amazon S3 object-level API activity (GetObject, DeleteObject, and PutObject API operations) or AWS Lambda function execution activity (the Invoke API). For more information, see Logging Data and Management Events for Trails.

Currently, GuardDuty only analyzes CloudTrail management events. If you have CloudTrail configured to log data events, there will be a difference between GuardDuty analysis based on CloudTrail data and the logs that CloudTrail itself is delivering.

Another important detail about GuardDuty's usage of CloudTrail as a data source is the handling and processing of CloudTrail's global events. For most services, events are recorded in the region where the action occurred. For global services such as AWS IAM, AWS STS, Amazon CloudFront, and Route 53, events are delivered to any trail that includes global services, and are logged as occurring in US East (N. Virginia) Region. For more information, see About Global Service Events.

GuardDuty processes all events that come into a region, including global events that CloudTrail sends to all regions. This allows GuardDuty to maintain user and role profiles in each region and enables it to accurately detect credentials that are being maliciously used across regions.

Important
It is highly recommended that you enable GuardDuty in all supported AWS regions. This allows GuardDuty to generate findings about unauthorized or unusual activity even in regions that you are not actively using. This also allows GuardDuty to monitor AWS CloudTrail events for global AWS services.
If GuardDuty is not enabled in all supported regions, its ability to detect activity that involves global services is reduced.
There is little to no additional cost for GuardDuty to monitor a region where you do not have active workloads deployed.

VPC Flow Logs

VPC Flow Logs capture information about the IP traffic going to and from Amazon EC2 network interfaces in your VPC. For more information, see VPC Flow Logs.

Important
When you enable GuardDuty, it immediately starts analyzing your VPC Flow Logs data. It consumes VPC Flow Log events directly from the VPC Flow Logs feature through an independent and duplicative stream of flow logs. This process does not affect any existing flow log configurations that you might have.
GuardDuty doesn't manage your flow logs or make them accessible in your account. To manage access and retention of your flow logs, you must configure the VPC Flow Logs feature.
There is no additional charge for GuardDuty access to flow logs. However, enabling flow logs for retention or use in your account falls under existing pricing. For more information, see Working With Flow Logs.

DNS logs

If you use AWS DNS resolvers for your EC2 instances (the default setting), then GuardDuty can access and process your request and response DNS logs through the internal AWS DNS resolvers. If you are using a 3rd party DNS resolver, for example, OpenDNS or GoogleDNS, or if you set up your own DNS resolvers, then GuardDuty cannot access and process data from this data source.

Amazon GuardDuty Terminology and Concepts

As you get started with Amazon GuardDuty, you can benefit from learning about its key concepts.

Account
A standard Amazon Web Services (AWS) account that contains your AWS resources. You can sign in to AWS with your account and enable GuardDuty.

You can also invite other accounts to enable GuardDuty and become associated with your AWS account in GuardDuty. If your invitations are accepted, your account is designated as the **master** GuardDuty account, and the added accounts become your **member** accounts. You can then view and manage those accounts' GuardDuty findings on their behalf.

Users of the master account can configure GuardDuty as well as view and manage GuardDuty findings for their own account and all of their member accounts. You can have up to 1000 member accounts in GuardDuty.

Users of member accounts can configure GuardDuty as well as view and manage GuardDuty findings in their account (either through the GuardDuty management console or GuardDuty API). Users of member accounts can't view or manage findings in other members' accounts.

An AWS account can't be a GuardDuty master and member account at the same time. An AWS account can accept only one membership invitation. Accepting a membership invitation is optional.

For more information, see Managing AWS Accounts in Amazon GuardDuty.

** Auto-archive**
Auto-archive rules allow you to create very specific combinations of attributes to suppress findings. For example, you can define a rule through the GuardDuty filter to auto-archive `Recon:EC2/Portscan` from only those instances in a specific VPC, running a specific AMI, or with a specific EC2 tag. This rule would result in port scan findings being automatically archived from the instances that meet the criteria. However, it still allows alerting if GuardDuty detects those instances conducting other malicious activity, such as crypto-currency mining.

Auto-archive rules defined in the GuardDuty master account apply to the GuardDuty member accounts. GuardDuty member accounts can't modify auto-archive rules.

With auto-archive rules, GuardDuty still generates all findings. Auto-archive rules provide suppression of findings while maintaining a complete and immutable history of all activity.

Data source
The origin or location of a set of data. To detect unauthorized and unexpected activity in your AWS environment, GuardDuty analyzes and processes data from AWS CloudTrail event logs, VPC Flow Logs, and DNS logs. For more information, see How Amazon GuardDuty Uses Its Data Sources.

Finding
A potential security issue discovered by GuardDuty. For more information, see Amazon GuardDuty Findings. Findings are displayed in the GuardDuty console and contain a detailed description of the security issue. You can also retrieve your generated findings by calling the GetFindings and ListFindings HTTPS API operations. You can also see your GuardDuty findings through Amazon CloudWatch events. GuardDuty sends findings to Amazon CloudWatch via HTTPS protocol. For more information, see Monitoring Amazon GuardDuty Findings with Amazon CloudWatch Events.

Trusted IP list
A list of whitelisted IP addresses for highly secure communication with your AWS environment. GuardDuty does not generate findings based on trusted IP lists. For more information, see Working with Trusted IP Lists and Threat Lists.

Threat list
A list of known malicious IP addresses. GuardDuty generates findings based on threat lists. For more information, see Working with Trusted IP Lists and Threat Lists.

Amazon GuardDuty Service Limits

The following are Amazon GuardDuty limits per AWS account per region:

Resource	Default Limit	Comments
Detectors	1	The maximum number of detector resources that can be created and activated per AWS account per region. This is a hard limit. You cannot request a limit increase of detectors.
Trusted IP sets	1	The maximum number of trusted IP sets that can be uploaded and activated per AWS account per region. This is a hard limit. You cannot request a limit increase of trusted IP sets.
Threat intel sets	6	The maximum number of threat intel sets that can be uploaded and activated per AWS account per region. This is a hard limit. You cannot request a limit increase of threat intel sets.
GuardDuty member accounts	1000	The maximum number of GuardDuty member accounts that can be added per AWS account (GuardDuty master account) per region. This is a hard limit. You cannot request a limit increase of member accounts.
GuardDuty finding retention time	90 days	The maximum number of days a GuardDuty-generated finding is saved. This is a hard limit. You cannot request a limit increase of finding retention days.

Amazon GuardDuty Supported Regions

Currently, Amazon GuardDuty is supported in the following AWS regions:

- Asia Pacific (Mumbai)
- Asia Pacific (Seoul)
- Asia Pacific (Singapore)
- Asia Pacific (Sydney)
- Asia Pacific (Tokyo)
- Canada (Central)
- EU (Frankfurt)
- EU (Ireland)
- EU (London)
- EU (Paris)
- US East (N. Virginia)
- US East (Ohio)
- US West (N. California)
- US West (Oregon)
- South America (São Paulo)

Important

It is highly recommended that you enable GuardDuty in all supported AWS regions. This allows GuardDuty to generate findings about unauthorized or unusual activity even in regions that you are not actively using. This also allows GuardDuty to monitor AWS CloudTrail events for global AWS services such as IAM.

If GuardDuty is not enabled in all supported regions, its ability to detect activity that involves global services is reduced.

There is little to no additional cost for GuardDuty to monitor a region where you do not have active workloads deployed.

Setting Up Amazon GuardDuty

You must have an AWS account in order to enable Amazon GuardDuty. If you don't have an account, use the following procedure to create one.

To sign up for AWS

1. Open https://aws.amazon.com/, and then choose **Create an AWS Account**. **Note**
   This might be unavailable in your browser if you previously signed into the AWS Management Console. In that case, choose **Sign in to a different account**, and then choose **Create a new AWS account**.

2. Follow the online instructions.

   Part of the sign-up procedure involves receiving a phone call and entering a PIN using the phone keypad.

Topics

- Enable Amazon GuardDuty
- Amazon GuardDuty Free Trial

Enable Amazon GuardDuty

To use GuardDuty, you must first enable it. Use the following procedure to enable GuardDuty.

1. The IAM identity (user, role, group) that you use to enable GuardDuty must have the required permissions. To grant the permissions required to enable GuardDuty, attach the following policy to an IAM user, group, or role: **Note**
   Replace the sample account ID in the example below with your actual AWS account ID.

```
 1  {
 2      "Version": "2012-10-17",
 3      "Statement": [
 4          {
 5              "Effect": "Allow",
 6              "Action": [
 7                  "guardduty:*"
 8              ],
 9              "Resource": "*"
10          },
11          {
12              "Effect": "Allow",
13              "Action": [
14                  "iam:CreateServiceLinkedRole"
15              ],
16              "Resource": "arn:aws:iam::123456789123:role/aws-service-role/guardduty.
                    amazonaws.com/AWSServiceRoleForAmazonGuardDuty",
17              "Condition": {
18                  "StringLike": {
19                      "iam:AWSServiceName": "guardduty.amazonaws.com"
20                  }
21              }
22          },
23
24      ]
25  }
```

2. Use the credentials of the IAM identity from step 1 to sign in to the GuardDuty console. When you open the GuardDuty console for the first time, choose **Get Started**, and then choose **Enable GuardDuty**.

Note the following about enabling GuardDuty:

- GuardDuty is assigned a service-linked role called `AWSServiceRoleForAmazonGuardDuty`. This service-linked role includes the permissions and trust policy that GuardDuty requires to consume and analyze events directly from AWS CloudTrail, VPC Flow Logs, and DNS logs and generate security findings. To view the details of `AWSServiceRoleForAmazonGuardDuty`, on the **Welcome to GuardDuty** page, choose **View service role permissions**. For more information, see Using a Service-Linked Role to Delegate Permissions to GuardDuty. For more information about service-linked roles, see Using Service-Linked Roles.
- After you enable GuardDuty, it immediately begins pulling and analyzing independent streams of data from AWS CloudTrail, VPC Flow Logs, and DNS logs to generate security findings. Because GuardDuty only consumes this data for purposes of determining if there are any findings, GuardDuty doesn't manage AWS CloudTrail, VPC Flow Logs, and DNS logs for you or make their events and logs available to you. If you have enabled these services independent of GuardDuty, you will continue to have the option to configure the settings of these data sources through their respective consoles or APIs. For more information about the data sources that GuardDuty integrates with, see What is AWS CloudTrail? and Working With Flow Logs. **Important**
  It is highly recommended that you enable GuardDuty in all supported AWS regions. This allows GuardDuty to generate findings about unauthorized or unusual activity even in regions that you are not actively using. This also allows GuardDuty to monitor AWS CloudTrail events for global AWS services such as IAM.
  If GuardDuty is not enabled in all supported regions, its ability to detect activity that involves global services is reduced.
  There is little to no additional cost for GuardDuty to monitor a region where you do not have active workloads deployed.
- You can disable GuardDuty at any time to stop it from processing and analyzing AWS CloudTrail events, VPC Flow Logs, and DNS logs. For more information, see Suspending or Disabling Amazon GuardDuty.

Amazon GuardDuty Free Trial

When you enable GuardDuty for the first time, your AWS account is automatically enrolled in a 30-day GuardDuty free trial. You can view the details of your GuardDuty free trial in the **Free trial** page of the GuardDuty console (choose **Free trial / Details** in the navigation pane). The details include your current position on the free trial timeline and the estimated daily cost for using GuardDuty after your free trial ends. This estimate is based on the logs that GuardDuty processes and analyzes daily during the free trial.

Important
This estimated daily cost does NOT project charges for using GuardDuty in all of the AWS accounts and regions where you enabled GuardDuty. The daily cost estimate is based only on the GuardDuty usage in the AWS account and the AWS region to which you're currently signed in.

You will not be charged for using GuardDuty until your free trial ends. For more information about GuardDuty pricing, see Amazon GuardDuty Pricing.

Managing Access to Amazon GuardDuty

Topics

- Permissions Required to Enable GuardDuty
- Using a Service-Linked Role to Delegate Permissions to GuardDuty
- Using IAM Policies to Delegate Access to GuardDuty to IAM Identities

Permissions Required to Enable GuardDuty

This section describes the permissions that various IAM identities (users, groups, and roles) must have in order to initially enable GuardDuty either through the console or programmatically (using the GuardDuty API or the GuardDuty commands in the AWS CLI).

To grant permissions required to enable GuardDuty, attach the following policy to an IAM user, group, or role:

Note

Replace the sample account ID in the example below with your actual AWS account ID.

```
1  {
2      "Version": "2012-10-17",
3      "Statement": [
4          {
5              "Effect": "Allow",
6              "Action": [
7                  "guardduty:*"
8              ],
9              "Resource": "*"
10         },
11         {
12             "Effect": "Allow",
13             "Action": [
14                 "iam:CreateServiceLinkedRole"
15             ],
16             "Resource": "arn:aws:iam::123456789012:role/aws-service-role/guardduty.amazonaws.com
                   /AWSServiceRoleForAmazonGuardDuty",
17             "Condition": {
18                 "StringLike": {
19                     "iam:AWSServiceName": "guardduty.amazonaws.com"
20                 }
21             }
22         },
23         {
24             "Effect": "Allow",
25             "Action": [
26                 "iam:PutRolePolicy",
27                 "iam:DeleteRolePolicy"
28             ],
29             "Resource": "arn:aws:iam::1234567890123:role/aws-service-role/guardduty.amazonaws.
                   com/AWSServiceRoleForAmazonGuardDuty"
30         }
31     ]
32 }
```

Using a Service-Linked Role to Delegate Permissions to GuardDuty

This section describes the permissions that the GuardDuty service itself requires to function and perform operations on your behalf, such as generating findings.

When you enable GuardDuty (using the GuardDuty console or programmatically through the API operations or AWS CLI commands), it is automatically assigned a service-linked role called `AWSServiceRoleForAmazonGuardDuty`. A service-linked role is a unique type of IAM role that is linked directly to an AWS service (in this case, GuardDuty). Service-linked roles are predefined by the service and include all the permissions that the service requires to call other AWS services on your behalf. The linked service (in this case, GuardDuty) also defines how you create, modify, and delete a service-linked role. For more information about service-linked roles, see Using Service-Linked Roles.

The `AWSServiceRoleForAmazonGuardDuty` service-linked role is created automatically when GuardDuty is enabled. It includes the permissions and the trust policies that GuardDuty requires to consume and analyze events directly from AWS CloudTrail, VPC Flow Logs, and DNS logs and generate security findings.

You cannot edit the `AWSServiceRoleForAmazonGuardDuty` service-linked role. You can view its permissions or delete this service-linked role via the IAM console. To delete the `AWSServiceRoleForAmazonGuardDuty` service-linked role, you must first disable GuardDuty in all regions in that AWS account.

To view the permissions attached to `AWSServiceRoleForAmazonGuardDuty`, choose the **View service role permissions** button in the **Setting/General** tab of the GuardDuty console.

The following is the permissions policy document that is attached to the `AWSServiceRoleForAmazonGuardDuty` service-linked role:

```
{
    "Version": "2012-10-17",
    "Statement": [
        {
            "Effect": "Allow",
            "Action": [
                "ec2:DescribeInstances",
                "ec2:DescribeImages"
            ],
            "Resource": "*"
        }
    ]
}
```

The following is the trust policy that is attached to the `AWSServiceRoleForAmazonGuardDuty` service-linked role:

```
{
  "Version": "2012-10-17",
  "Statement": [
    {
      "Effect": "Allow",
      "Principal": {
        "Service": "guardduty.amazonaws.com"
      },
      "Action": "sts:AssumeRole"
    }
  ]
}
```

Using IAM Policies to Delegate Access to GuardDuty to IAM Identities

This section describes how to delegate access to GuardDuty to various IAM identities (users, groups, and roles).

By default, access to the GuardDuty resources (detector, trusted IP lists, threat lists, findings, members, master account, and invitations) is restricted to the owner of the AWS account that the resources were created in. If you are the owner, you can choose to grant full or limited access to GuardDuty to the various IAM identities in your account. For more information about creating IAM access policies, see AWS Identity and Access Management (IAM).

Topics

- AWS Managed (Predefined) Policies for GuardDuty
- Using a Custom IAM Policy to Grant Full Access to GuardDuty
- Using a Custom IAM Policy to Grant Read-only Access to GuardDuty
- Using a Custom IAM Policy to Deny Access to GuardDuty Findings
- Using a Custom IAM Policy to Limit Access to GuardDuty Resources

AWS Managed (Predefined) Policies for GuardDuty

AWS addresses many common use cases by providing standalone IAM policies that are created and administered by AWS. These *managed policies* grant necessary permissions for common use cases so that you can avoid having to investigate which permissions are needed. For more information, see AWS Managed Policies in the *IAM User Guide*.

The following AWS managed policies, which you can attach to users in your account, are specific to GuardDuty:

- **AmazonGuardDutyFullAccess ** – provides access to all of GuardDuty functionality. However, when it comes to working with trusted IP lists and threat lists in GuardDuty, this managed policy provides identities with only limited access. More specifically, an identity with the **AmazonGuardDutyFullAccess** managed policy attached can only rename and deactivate uploaded trusted IP lists and threat lists.

  To grant various identities full access to working with trusted IP lists and threat lists (in addition to renaming and deactivating, this includes uploading, activating, deleting, and updating the location of the lists), make sure that the following actions are present in the permissions policy attached to an IAM user, group, or role:

```
1        {
2            "Effect": "Allow",
3            "Action": [
4                "iam:PutRolePolicy",
5                "iam:DeleteRolePolicy"
6            ],
7            "Resource": "arn:aws:iam::123456789123:role/aws-service-role/guardduty.
                 amazonaws.com/AWSServiceRoleForAmazonGuardDuty"
8        }
```

- **AmazonGuardDutyReadOnlyAccess ** – Provides read-only access to GuardDuty.

Using a Custom IAM Policy to Grant Full Access to GuardDuty

You can use the following custom policy to grant an IAM user, role, or group full access to the GuardDuty console and all GuardDuty operations.

Note
Replace the sample account ID in the example below with your actual AWS account ID.

```
 1 {
 2     "Version": "2012-10-17",
 3     "Statement": [
 4         {
 5             "Effect": "Allow",
 6             "Action": [
 7                 "guardduty:*"
 8             ],
 9             "Resource": "*"
10         },
11         {
12             "Effect": "Allow",
13             "Action": [
14                 "iam:CreateServiceLinkedRole"
15             ],
16             "Resource": "arn:aws:iam::123456789123:role/aws-service-role/guardduty.amazonaws.com
                /AWSServiceRoleForAmazonGuardDuty",
17             "Condition": {
18                 "StringLike": {
19                     "iam:AWSServiceName": "guardduty.amazonaws.com"
20                 }
21             }
22         },
23         {
24             "Effect": "Allow",
25             "Action": [
26                 "iam:PutRolePolicy",
27                 "iam:DeleteRolePolicy"
28             ],
29             "Resource": "arn:aws:iam::123456789123:role/aws-service-role/guardduty.amazonaws.com
                /AWSServiceRoleForAmazonGuardDuty"
30         }
31     ]
32 }
```

Using a Custom IAM Policy to Grant Read-only Access to GuardDuty

You can use the following policy to grant an IAM user, role, or group read-only access to GuardDuty:

```
 1 {
 2     "Version": "2012-10-17",
 3     "Statement": [
 4         {
 5             "Effect": "Allow",
 6             "Action": [
 7                 "guardduty:ListMembers",
 8                 "guardduty:GetMembers",
 9                 "guardduty:ListInvitations",
10                 "guardduty:ListDetectors",
11                 "guardduty:GetDetector",
12                 "guardduty:ListFindings",
13                 "guardduty:GetFindings",
14                 "guardduty:ListIPSets",
15                 "guardduty:GetIPSet",
```

```
16            "guardduty:ListThreatIntelSets",
17            "guardduty:GetThreatIntelSet",
18            "guardduty:GetMasterAccount",
19            "guardduty:GetInvitationsCount",
20            "guardduty:GetFindingsStatistics"
21          ],
22          "Resource": "*"
23        }
24      ]
25  }
```

Using a Custom IAM Policy to Deny Access to GuardDuty Findings

You can use the following policy to deny an IAM user, role, or group access to GuardDuty findings. Users can't view findings or the details about findings, but they can access all other GuardDuty operations:

```
1  {
2      "Version": "2012-10-17",
3      "Statement": [
4          {
5              "Effect": "Allow",
6              "Action": [
7                  "guardduty:CreateDetector",
8                  "guardduty:DeleteDetector",
9                  "guardduty:UpdateDetector",
10                 "guardduty:GetDetector",
11                 "guardduty:ListDetectors",
12                 "guardduty:CreateIPSet",
13                 "guardduty:DeleteIPSet",
14                 "guardduty:UpdateIPSet",
15                 "guardduty:GetIPSet",
16                 "guardduty:ListIPSets",
17                 "guardduty:CreateThreatIntelSet",
18                 "guardduty:DeleteThreatIntelSet",
19                 "guardduty:UpdateThreatIntelSet",
20                 "guardduty:GetThreatIntelSet",
21                 "guardduty:ListThreatIntelSets",
22                 "guardduty:ArchiveFindings",
23                 "guardduty:UnarchiveFindings",
24                 "guardduty:CreateSampleFindings",
25                 "guardduty:CreateMembers",
26                 "guardduty:InviteMembers",
27                 "guardduty:GetMembers",
28                 "guardduty:DeleteMembers",
29                 "guardduty:DisassociateMembers",
30                 "guardduty:StartMonitoringMembers",
31                 "guardduty:StopMonitoringMembers",
32                 "guardduty:ListMembers",
33                 "guardduty:GetMasterAccount",
34                 "guardduty:DisassociateFromMasterAccount",
35                 "guardduty:AcceptInvitation",
36                 "guardduty:ListInvitations",
37                 "guardduty:GetInvitationsCount",
38                 "guardduty:DeclineInvitations",
```

```
39              "guardduty:DeleteInvitations"
40          ],
41          "Resource": "*"
42      },
43      {
44          "Effect": "Allow",
45          "Action": [
46              "iam:CreateServiceLinkedRole"
47          ],
48          "Resource": "arn:aws:iam::123456789123:role/aws-service-role/guardduty.amazonaws.com
                /AWSServiceRoleForAmazonGuardDuty",
49          "Condition": {
50              "StringLike": {
51                  "iam:AWSServiceName": "guardduty.amazonaws.com"
52              }
53          }
54      },
55      {
56          "Effect": "Allow",
57          "Action": [
58              "iam:PutRolePolicy",
59              "iam:DeleteRolePolicy"
60          ],
61          "Resource": "arn:aws:iam::123456789123:role/aws-service-role/guardduty.amazonaws.com
                /AWSServiceRoleForAmazonGuardDuty"
62      }
63  ]
64 }
```

Using a Custom IAM Policy to Limit Access to GuardDuty Resources

To define a user's access to GuardDuty based on the detector ID, you can use all GuardDuty operations in your custom IAM policies, **except** the following operations:

- guardduty:CreateDetector
- guardduty:DeclineInvitations
- guardduty:DeleteInvitations
- guardduty:GetInvitationsCount
- guardduty:ListDetectors
- guardduty:ListInvitations

Use the following operations in an IAM policy to define a user's access to GuardDuty based on the IPSet ID and ThreatIntelSet ID:

- guardduty:DeleteIPSet
- guardduty:DeleteThreatIntelSet
- guardduty:GetIPSet
- guardduty:GetThreatIntelSet
- guardduty:UpdateIPSet
- guardduty:UpdateThreatIntelSet

The following examples show how to create policies using some of the preceding operations:

- This policy allows a user to run the guardduty:UpdateDetector operation, using the detector ID of 1234567 in the us-east-1 region:

```
1  {
2      "Version": "2012-10-17",
3      "Statement": [
4          {
5              "Effect": "Allow",
6              "Action": [
7                  "guardduty:UpdateDetector",
8              ],
9              "Resource": "arn:aws:guardduty:us-east-1:012345678910:detector/1234567"
10         }
11     ]
12 }
```

- This policy allows a user to run the `guardduty:UpdateIPSet` operation, using the detector ID of 1234567 and the IPSet ID of 000000 in the us-east-1 region: **Note**
  Make sure that the user has the permissions required to access trusted IP lists and threat lists in GuardDuty. For more information, see Permissions Required to Upload Trusted IP Lists and Threat Lists.

```
1  {
2      "Version": "2012-10-17",
3      "Statement": [
4          {
5              "Effect": "Allow",
6              "Action": [
7                  "guardduty:UpdateIPSet",
8              ],
9              "Resource": "arn:aws:guardduty:us-east-1:012345678910:detector/1234567/ipset
                   /000000"
10         }
11     ]
12 }
```

- This policy allows a user to run the `guardduty:UpdateIPSet` operation, using any detector ID and the IPSet ID of 000000 in the us-east-1 region: **Note**
  Make sure that the user has the permissions required to access trusted IP lists and threat lists in GuardDuty. For more information, see Permissions Required to Upload Trusted IP Lists and Threat Lists.

```
1  {
2      "Version": "2012-10-17",
3      "Statement": [
4          {
5              "Effect": "Allow",
6              "Action": [
7                  "guardduty:UpdateIPSet",
8              ],
9              "Resource": "arn:aws:guardduty:us-east-1:012345678910:detector/*/ipset/000000"
10         }
11     ]
12 }
```

- This policy allows a user to run the `guardduty:UpdateIPSet` operation, using the detector ID of 1234567 and any IPSet ID in the us-east-1 region: **Note**
  Make sure that the user has the permissions required to access trusted IP lists and threat lists in GuardDuty. For more information, see Permissions Required to Upload Trusted IP Lists and Threat Lists.

```
1  {
```

```
 2      "Version": "2012-10-17",
 3      "Statement": [
 4          {
 5              "Effect": "Allow",
 6              "Action": [
 7                  "guardduty:UpdateIPSet",
 8              ],
 9              "Resource": "arn:aws:guardduty:us-east-1:012345678910:detector/1234567/ipset/*"
10          }
11      ]
12  }
```

Amazon GuardDuty Findings

Amazon GuardDuty generates findings when it detects unexpected and potentially malicious activity in your AWS environment. You can view and manage your GuardDuty findings on the **Findings** page in the GuardDuty console or by using the GuardDuty CLI or API operations. You can also view your GuardDuty findings through Amazon CloudWatch events. For more information, see Monitoring Amazon GuardDuty Findings with Amazon CloudWatch Events.

This topic describes the following information:

Topics

- Locating and Analyzing GuardDuty Findings
- Archiving, Exporting, and Providing Feedback on GuardDuty Findings
- Filtering and Auto-Archiving GuardDuty Findings
- Severity Levels for GuardDuty Findings
- Generating GuardDuty Sample Findings
- Proof of Concept - Automatically Generating Several Common GuardDuty Findings
- Amazon GuardDuty Finding Types
- Remediating Security Issues Discovered by Amazon GuardDuty

Locating and Analyzing GuardDuty Findings

Use the following procedure to view and analyze your GuardDuty findings.

---

1. Open the GuardDuty console at https://console.aws.amazon.com/guardduty, and then choose **Findings**.

2. Choose a specific finding to view its details.

   A details pane appears where you can view the following information:

   - A finding's summary section that includes the following information:
     - **Finding type** – a concise yet readable description of the potential security issue. For more information, see Amazon GuardDuty Finding Types.
     - **Severity** – a finding's assigned severity level of either High, Medium, or Low. For more information, see Severity Levels for GuardDuty Findings.
     - **Region** – the AWS region in which the finding was generated. **Note** For more information about supported regions, see Amazon GuardDuty Supported Regions
     - **Count** – the number of times GuardDuty generated the finding after you enabled GuardDuty in your AWS account.
     - **Account ID** – the ID of the AWS account in which the activity took place that prompted GuardDuty to generate this finding.
     - **Resource ID** – the ID of the AWS resource against which the activity took place that prompted GuardDuty to generate this finding.
     - **Threat list name** - the name of the threat list that includes the IP address or the domain name involved in the activity that prompted GuardDuty to generate the finding.
     - **Last seen** – the time at which the activity took place that prompted GuardDuty to generate this finding. **Note** Findings' time stamps in the GuardDuty console appear in your local time zone, while JSON exports and CLI outputs display timestamps in UTC.
   - A finding's **Resource affected** section that includes the following information:
     - **Resource role** – a value that usually is set to **Target ** because the affected resource can be a potential target of an attack.
     - **Resource type** – the type of the affected resource. This value is either **AccessKey** or **Instance**. Currently, supported finding types highlight potentially malicious activity against either EC2

28

instances or AWS credentials. For more information, see Remediating Security Issues Discovered by Amazon GuardDuty.

- **Instance ID** – the ID of the EC2 instance involved in the activity that prompted GuardDuty to generate the finding.
- **Port** – the port number for the connection used during the activity that prompted GuardDuty to generate the finding.
- **Access key ID** – access key ID of the user engaged in the activity that prompted GuardDuty to generate the finding.
- **Principal ID** – the principal ID of the user engaged in the activity that prompted GuardDuty to generate the finding.
- **User type** – the type of user engaged in the activity that prompted GuardDuty to generate the finding. For more information, see CloudTrail userIdentity element.
- **User name** – The name of the user engaged in the activity that prompted GuardDuty to generate the finding.

- A finding's **Action** section that can include the following information:
  - **Action type** – the finding activity type. This value can be one of the following: NETWORK_CONNECTION, AWS_API_CALL, PORT_PROBE, or DNS_REQUEST. NETWORK_CONNECTION indicates that network traffic was exchanged between the identified EC2 instance and the remote host. AWS_API_CALL indicates that an AWS API was invoked. DNS_REQUEST indicates that the identified EC2 instance queried a domain name. PORT_PROBE indicates that a remote host probed the identified EC2 instance on multiple open ports.
  - **API** – the name of the API operation that was invoked and thus prompted GuardDuty to generate this finding.
  - **Service name** – the name of the AWS service (GuardDuty) that generated the finding.
  - **Connection direction** – the network connection direction observed in the activity that prompted GuardDuty to generate the finding. The values can be INBOUND, OUTBOUND, and UNKNOWN. INBOUND indicates that a remote host initiated a connection to a local port on the identified EC2 instance in your account. OUTBOUND indicates that the identified EC2 instance initiated a connection to a remote host. UNKNOWN indicates that GuardDuty could not determine the direction of the connection.
  - **Protocol** – the network connection protocol observed in the activity that prompted GuardDuty to generate the finding.

- A finding's **Actor** section that can include the following information:
  - **Location** – location information of the IP address involved in the activity that prompted GuardDuty to generate the finding.
  - **Organization** – ISP organization information of the IP address involved in the activity that prompted GuardDuty to generate the finding.
  - **IP address** – the IP address involved in the activity that prompted GuardDuty to generate the finding.
  - **Port** – the port number involved in the activity that prompted GuardDuty to generate the finding.
  - **Domain** – the domain involved in the activity that prompted GuardDuty to generate the finding.

- A finding's **Additional information** section that can include the following information:
  - **Threat list name** – the name of the threat list that includes the IP address or the domain name involved in the activity that prompted GuardDuty to generate the finding.
  - **Sample** – indicates whether this is a sample finding.
  - **Unusual** – activity details that were not observed historically. These can include an unusual (previously not observed) user, or location, or time.
  - ****Unusual protocol ****– the network connection protocol involved in the activity that prompted GuardDuty to generate the finding.

Archiving, Exporting, and Providing Feedback on GuardDuty Findings

Use the following procedure to archive your findings or mark them as current and to provide feedback for your GuardDuty findings

---

1. To archive or export a finding, choose it from the list of your findings and then choose the **Actions** menu. Then choose **Archive** or **Export**. When you **Export** a finding, you can see its full JSON document. **Note**
   Currently in GuardDuty, users from GuardDuty member accounts CANNOT archive findings. **Note**
   If and only if the confidence level of a GuardDuty finding is set to 0, you the **Confidence** field is displayed in the full finding JSON. The presence of the **Confidence** field set to 0 indicates that this GuardDuty finding is a false positive.

2. To provide feedback by marking the finding useful or not useful, choose it from the list of your findings and then choose the thumbs up or thumbs down icons.

Filtering and Auto-Archiving GuardDuty Findings

Use the following procedure to create filters for your GuardDuty findings.

---

1. Choose the **Add filter criteria** bar above the displayed list of your GuardDuty findings.

2. In the expanded list of attributes, select the attributes that you want to specify as the criteria for your filter. For example, **Account ID** and/or **Action type**. You can specify one attribute or a maximum of 50 attributes as the criteria for a particular filter.

   For the complete list of attributes that you can specify as filter criteria, see the details of the filterCriteria property in CreateFilter.

3. In the displayed text field, specify a value for each selected attribute and then select **Apply**. **Note**
   In a particular filter, for the attributes where you're using the 'equal to' or 'not equal to' condition to be applied to the attribute value, (for example, Account ID), you can specify up to a maximum of 50 values.

4. To save the specified attributes and their values (filter criteria) as a filter, select **Save**. Provide the filter name and description, and use the **Auto-archive** checkbox to specify whether the findings that match this filter are to be automatically archived. Then select **Done**. For more information, see Auto-archive.

Severity Levels for GuardDuty Findings

Each GuardDuty finding has an assigned severity level and value that reduces the need to prioritize one finding over another and can help you determine your response to a potential security issue that is highlighted by a finding. The value of the severity can fall anywhere within the 0.1 to 8.9 range.

Note
Values 0 and 9.0 to 10.0 are currently reserved for future use.

The following are the currently defined severity levels and values for the GuardDuty findings:

- **High** (the value of the **severity** parameter in the GetFindings response falls within the 7.0 to 8.9 range) – indicates that the resource in question (an EC2 instance or a set of IAM user credentials) is compromised and is actively being used for unauthorized purposes. We recommend that you treat this security issue as a priority and take immediate remediation steps. For example, clean up your EC2 instance or terminate it, or rotate the IAM credentials.

- **Medium** (the value of the **severity** parameter in the GetFindings response falls within the 4.0 to 6.9 range) – indicates suspicious activity, for example, a large amount of traffic being returned to a remote host that is hiding behind the Tor network, or activity that deviates from normally observed behavior. We recommend that you investigate the implicated resource at your earliest convenience. Here are some of the possible remediation steps:
  - Check if an authorized user has installed new software that changed the behavior of a resource (for example, allowed higher than normal traffic, or enabled communication on a new port).
  - Check if an authorized user changed the control panel settings, for example, modified a security group setting
  - Run an anti-virus scan on the implicated resource to detect unauthorized software.
  - Verify the permissions that are attached to the implicated IAM role, user, group, or set of credentials. These might have to be changed or rotated.
- **Low** (the value of the **severity** parameter in the GetFindings response falls within the 0.1 to 3.9 range) - indicates suspicious or malicious activity that was blocked before it compromised your resource. There is no immediate recommended action, but it is worth making note of this information as something to address in the future.

Generating GuardDuty Sample Findings

Sample findings can help you visualize and analyze the various finding types that GuardDuty generates. When you generate sample findings, GuardDuty populates your current findings list with one sample finding for each supported finding type. For more information about GuardDuty finding types, see Amazon GuardDuty Finding Types.

Use the following procedure to generate sample findings.

1. Open the GuardDuty console at https://console.aws.amazon.com/guardduty.

2. In the navigation pane, under **Settings**, choose **General**.

3. On the **Settings** page, under **Sample findings**, choose **Generate sample findings**.

4. In the navigation pane, under **Findings**, choose **Current**. The sample findings are displayed on the **Current findings** page. The title of sample findings always begins with [**SAMPLE**]. Choose a specific sample finding to view its details.

Proof of Concept - Automatically Generating Several Common GuardDuty Findings

You can use the following scripts to automatically generate several common Amazon GuardDuty findings. **guardduty-tester.template** uses AWS CloudFormation to create an isolated environment with a bastion host, a tester EC2 instance that you can ssh into, and two target EC2 instances. Then you can run **guardduty_tester.sh** that starts interaction between the tester EC2 instance and the target Windows EC2 instance and the target Linux EC2 instance to simulate five types of common attacks that GuardDuty is built to detect and notify you about with generated findings.

1. As a prerequisite, you must enable GuardDuty in the same account and region where you want to run the **guardduty-tester.template** and **guardduty_tester.sh**. For more information about enabling GuardDuty, see Setting Up Amazon GuardDuty.

   You must also generate a new or use an existing EC2 key pair in each region where you want to run these scripts. This EC2 key pair is used as a parameter in the **guardduty-tester.template** script that you use to create a new CloudFormation stack. For more information about generating EC2 key pairs, see https://docs.aws.amazon.com/AWSEC2/latest/UserGuide/ec2-key-pairs.html.

2. Create a new CloudFormation stack using **guardduty-tester.template**. For detailed instructions about creating a stack, see https://docs.aws.amazon.com/AWSCloudFormation/latest/UserGuide/cfn-console-create-stack.html. Before you run **guardduty-tester.template**, modify it with values for the following parameters: Stack Name to identify your new stack, Availability Zone where you want to run the stack, and Key Pair that you can use to launch the EC2 instances. Then you can use the corresponding private key to SSH into the EC2 instances.

   guardduty-tester.template takes around 10 minutes to run and complete. It creates your environment and copies **guardduty_tester.sh** onto your tester EC2 instance.

3. In the AWS CloudFormation console, choose the checkbox next to your new running CloudFormation stack. In the displayed set of tabs, select the **Output** tab. Note the IP addresses assigned to the bastion host and the tester EC2 instance. You need both of these IP addresses in order to ssh into the tester EC2 instance.

4. Create the following entry in your ~/.ssh/config file to login to your instance through the bastion host:

```
1 Host bastion
2     HostName {Elastic IP Address of Bastion}
3     User ec2-user
4     IdentityFile ~/.ssh/{your-ssh-key.pem}
5 Host tester
6     ForwardAgent yes
7     HostName {Local IP Address of RedTeam Instance}
8     User ec2-user
9     IdentityFile ~/.ssh/{your-ssh-key.pem
10    ProxyCommand ssh bastion nc %h %p
11    ServerAliveInterval 240
```

   Now you can call $ ssh tester to login to your target EC2 instance. For more information about configuring and connecting to EC2 instances through bastion hosts, see https://aws.amazon.com/blogs/security/securely-connect-to-linux-instances-running-in-a-private-amazon-vpc/.

5. Once connected to the tester EC2 instance, run **guardduty_tester.sh** to initiate interaction between your tester and target EC2 instances, simulate attacks, and generate GuardDuty Findings.

Amazon GuardDuty Finding Types

Topics

- Finding Type Format
- Complete List of GuardDuty Active Finding Types
- Complete List of GuardDuty Retired Finding Types

Finding Type Format

When GuardDuty detects suspicious or unexpected behavior in your AWS environment, it generates a finding. A finding is a notification that contains the details about a potential security issue that GuardDuty discovers. The finding details include information about what happened, what AWS resources were involved in the suspicious activity, when this activity took place, and other information.

One of the most useful pieces of information in the finding details is a **finding type**. The purpose of the finding type is to provide a concise yet readable description of the potential security issue. For example, the GuardDuty *Recon:EC2/PortProbeUnprotectedPort* finding type quickly informs you that somewhere in your AWS environment, an EC2 instance has an unprotected port that a potential attacker is probing.

GuardDuty uses the following format for the various finding types that it generates:

ThreatPurpose:ResourceTypeAffected/ThreatFamilyName.ThreatFamilyVariant!Artifact

This is what each part of the format represents:

- **ThreatPurpose** - describes the primary purpose of a threat or a potential attack. In the current release of GuardDuty, ThreatPurpose can have the following values:
    - **Backdoor** - this value indicates that the attack has compromised an AWS resource and is capable of contacting its home command and control (C&C) server to receive further instructions for malicious activity.
    - **Behavior** - this value indicates that GuardDuty is detecting activity or activity patterns that are different from the established baseline for a particular AWS resource.
    - **Cryptocurrency** - this value indicates that GuardDuty is detecting software that is associated with cryptocurrencies (for example, Bitcoin).
    - **Pentest **- Sometimes owners of AWS resources or their authorized representatives intentionally run tests against AWS applications to find vulnerabilities, like open security groups or access keys that are overly permissive. These pen tests are done in an attempt to identify and lock down vulnerable resources before they are discovered by attackers. However, some of the tools used by authorized pen testers are freely available, and therefore can be used by unauthorized users or attackers to run probing tests. Although GuardDuty can't identify the true purpose behind such activity, the **Pentest** value indicates that GuardDuty is detecting such activity and that it is similar to the activity generated by known pen testing tools. Therefore, it can be a potential attack.
    - **Persistence **- this value indicates that an IAM user in your AWS environment is exhibiting behavior that is different from the established baseline. For example, this IAM user has no prior history of updating network configuration settings, or updating policies or permissions attached to AWS users or resources.
    - **Recon **- this value indicates that a reconnaissance attack is underway, scoping out vulnerabilities in your AWS environment by probing ports, listing users, database tables, and so on.
    - **ResourceConsumption **- this value indicates that an IAM user in your AWS environment is exhibiting behavior that is different from the established baseline. For example, this IAM user has no prior history of launching EC2 instances.
    - **Stealth **- this value indicates that an attack is actively trying to hide its actions and its tracks. For example, an attack might use an anonymizing proxy server, making it virtually impossible to gauge the true nature of the activity.

- **Trojan** - this value indicates that an attack is using Trojan programs that silently carry out malicious activity. Sometimes this software takes on an appearance of a legitimate program. Sometimes users accidentally run this software. Other times this software might run automatically by exploiting a vulnerability.
  - **UnauthorizedAccess** - this value indicates that GuardDuty is detecting suspicious activity or a suspicious activity pattern by an unauthorized individual.
- **ResourceTypeAffected** - describes which AWS resource is identified in this finding as the potential target of an attack. In this release of GuardDuty, only EC2 instances and IAM users (and their credentials) can be identified as affected resources in GuardDuty findings.
- **ThreatFamilyName** - describes the overall threat or potential malicious activity that GuardDuty is detecting. For example, a value of **NetworkPortUnusual** indicates that an EC2 instance identified in the GuardDuty finding has no prior history of communications on a particular remote port that also is identified in the finding.
- **ThreatFamilyVariant** - describes the specific variant of the **ThreatFamily** that GuardDuty is detecting. Attackers often slightly modify the functionality of the attack, thus creating new variants.
- **Artifact** - describes a specific resource that is owned by a tool that is used in the attack. For example, **DNS** in the finding type *CryptoCurrency:EC2/BitcoinTool.B!DNS* indicates that an EC2 instance is communicating with a known Bitcoin-related domain.

Complete List of GuardDuty Active Finding Types

The following are various finding types that GuardDuty generates:

Topics

- Backdoor:EC2/XORDDOS
- Backdoor:EC2/Spambot
- Backdoor:EC2/C&CActivity.B!DNS
- Behavior:EC2/NetworkPortUnusual
- Behavior:EC2/TrafficVolumeUnusual
- CryptoCurrency:EC2/BitcoinTool.B!DNS
- PenTest:IAMUser/KaliLinux
- Persistence:IAMUser/NetworkPermissions
- Persistence:IAMUser/ResourcePermissions
- Persistence:IAMUser/UserPermissions
- Recon:EC2/PortProbeUnprotectedPort
- Recon:IAMUser/TorIPCaller
- Recon:IAMUser/MaliciousIPCaller.Custom
- Recon:IAMUser/MaliciousIPCaller
- Recon:EC2/Portscan
- Recon:IAMUser/NetworkPermissions
- Recon:IAMUser/ResourcePermissions
- Recon:IAMUser/UserPermissions
- ResourceConsumption:IAMUser/ComputeResources
- Stealth:IAMUser/PasswordPolicyChange
- Stealth:IAMUser/CloudTrailLoggingDisabled
- Stealth:IAMUser/LoggingConfigurationModified
- Trojan:EC2/BlackholeTraffic
- Trojan:EC2/DropPoint
- Trojan:EC2/BlackholeTraffic!DNS
- Trojan:EC2/DriveBySourceTraffic!DNS
- Trojan:EC2/DropPoint!DNS
- Trojan:EC2/DGADomainRequest.B
- Trojan:EC2/DGADomainRequest.C!DNS
- Trojan:EC2/DNSDataExfiltration

- Trojan:EC2/PhishingDomainRequest!DNS
- UnauthorizedAccess:IAMUser/TorIPCaller
- UnauthorizedAccess:IAMUser/MaliciousIPCaller.Custom
- UnauthorizedAccess:IAMUser/ConsoleLoginSuccess.B
- UnauthorizedAccess:IAMUser/MaliciousIPCaller
- UnauthorizedAccess:IAMUser/UnusualASNCaller
- UnauthorizedAccess:EC2/TorIPCaller
- UnauthorizedAccess:EC2/MaliciousIPCaller.Custom
- UnauthorizedAccess:EC2/SSHBruteForce
- UnauthorizedAccess:EC2/RDPBruteForce
- UnauthorizedAccess:IAMUser/InstanceCredentialExfiltration
- UnauthorizedAccess:IAMUser/ConsoleLogin

Backdoor:EC2/XORDDOS

Finding description

An EC2 instance is attempting to communicate with an IP address that is associated with XorD-Dos malware.

This finding informs you that an EC2 instance in your AWS environment is attempting to communicate with an IP address that is associated with XorDDos malware. This EC2 instance might be compromised. XOR DDoS is Trojan malware that hijacks Linux systems. To gain access to the system, it launches a brute force attack in order to discover the password to Secure Shell (SSH) services on Linux. After SSH credentials are acquired and the login is successful, it uses root privileges to run a script that downloads and installs XOR DDoS. This malware is then used as part of a botnet to launch distributed denial of service (DDoS) attacks against other targets. For more information, see Remediating a Compromised EC2 Instance.

Backdoor:EC2/Spambot

Finding description

EC2 instance is exhibiting unusual behavior by communicating with a remote host on port 25.

This finding informs you that an EC2 instance in your AWS environment is communicating with a remote host on port 25. This behavior is unusual because this EC2 instance has no prior history of communications on port 25. Port 25 is traditionally used by mail servers for SMTP communications. Your EC2 instance might be compromised and sending out spam. For more information, see Remediating a Compromised EC2 Instance.

Backdoor:EC2/C&CActivity.B!DNS

Finding description

EC2 instance is querying a domain name that is associated with a known command and control server.

This finding informs you that there is an EC2 instance in your AWS environment that is querying a domain name associated with a known command and control (C&C) server. Your EC2 instance might be compromised. C&C servers are computers that issue commands to members of a botnet. A botnet is a collection of internet-connected devices (which might include PCs, servers, mobile devices, and internet of things devices) that are infected and controlled by a common type of malware. Botnets are often used to distribute malware and gather misappropriated information, such as credit card numbers. Depending on the purpose and structure of the botnet, the C&C server might also issue commands to begin a distributed denial of service (DDoS) attack. For more information, see Remediating a Compromised EC2 Instance.

To test how GuardDuty's generates this finding type you can make a DNS request against a test domain
guarddutyc2activityb.com.

Behavior:EC2/NetworkPortUnusual

Finding description

EC2 instance is communicating with a remote host on an unusual server port.

This finding informs you that an EC2 instance in your AWS environment is behaving in a way that deviates from the established baseline. This EC2 instance has no prior history of communications on this remote port. Your EC2 instance might be compromised. For more information, see Remediating a Compromised EC2 Instance.

Behavior:EC2/TrafficVolumeUnusual

Finding description

EC2 instance is generating unusually large amounts of network traffic to a remote host.

This finding informs you that an EC2 instance in your AWS environment is behaving in a way that deviates from the established baseline. This EC2 instance has no prior history of sending this much traffic to this remote host. Your EC2 instance might be compromised. For more information, see Remediating a Compromised EC2 Instance.

CryptoCurrency:EC2/BitcoinTool.B!DNS

Finding description

EC2 instance is querying a domain name that is associated with Bitcoin-related activity.

This finding informs you that an EC2 instance in your AWS environment is querying a domain name that is associated with Bitcoin-related activity. Bitcoin is a worldwide cryptocurrency and digital payment system. Besides being created as a reward for Bitcoin mining, bitcoin can be exchanged for other currencies, products, and services. Unless you use this EC2 instance to mine or manage cryptocurrency or your EC2 instance is involved in blockchain activity, your EC2 instance might be compromised. For more information, see Remediating a Compromised EC2 Instance.

PenTest:IAMUser/KaliLinux

Finding description

An API was invoked from a Kali Linux EC2 instance.

This finding informs you that a machine running Kali Linux is making API calls using credentials that belong to your AWS account. Your credentials might be compromised. Kali Linux is a popular penetration testing tool used by security professionals to identify weaknesses in EC2 instances that require patching. This tool is also used by attackers to find EC2 configuration weaknesses and gain unauthorized access to your AWS environment. For more information, see Remediating Compromised AWS Credentials.

Persistence:IAMUser/NetworkPermissions

Finding description

An IAM user invoked an API commonly used to change the network access permissions for security groups, routes, and ACLs in your AWS account.

This finding informs you that a specific IAM user in your AWS environment is exhibiting behavior that is different from the established baseline. This IAM user has no prior history of invoking this API. Your credentials might be compromised. For more information, see Remediating Compromised AWS Credentials.

This finding is triggered when network configuration settings are changed under suspicious circumstances. For example, if an IAM user in your AWS environment with no prior history of doing so, invoked the CreateSecurity-Group API. Attackers often attempt to change security groups, allowing certain inbound traffic on various ports in order to improve their ability to access the bot they might have planted on your EC2 instance.

Persistence:IAMUser/ResourcePermissions

Finding description

An IAM user invoked an API commonly used to change the security access policies of various resources in your AWS account.

This finding informs you that a specific IAM user in your AWS environment is exhibiting behavior that is different from the established baseline. This IAM user has no prior history of invoking this API. Your credentials might be compromised. For more information, see Remediating Compromised AWS Credentials.

This finding is triggered when a change is detected to policies or permissions attached to AWS resources. For example, if an IAM user in your AWS environment with no prior history of doing so, invoked the PutBucketPolicy API. Some services, for example, Amazon S3, support resource-attached permissions that grant one or more IAM principals access to the resource. With stolen credentials, attackers can change the policies attached to a resource, granting themselves future access to that resource.

Persistence:IAMUser/UserPermissions

Finding description

An IAM user invoked an API commonly used to add, modify, or delete IAM users, groups or policies in your AWS account.

This finding informs you that a specific IAM user in your AWS environment is exhibiting behavior that is different from the established baseline. This IAM user has no prior history of invoking this API. Your credentials might be compromised. For more information, see Remediating Compromised AWS Credentials.

This finding is triggered by suspicious changes to the user-related permissions in your AWS environment. For example, if an IAM user in your AWS environment with no prior history of doing so, invoked the AttachUserPolicy API. In an effort to maximize their ability to access the account even after they have been discovered, attackers can use stolen credentials to create new users, add access policies to existing users, create access keys, etc. The owner of the account might notice that a particular IAM user or password was stolen and delete it from the account, but might not delete other users that were created by the fraudulently created admin IAM user, leaving their AWS account still accessible to the attacker.

Recon:EC2/PortProbeUnprotectedPort

Finding description

**EC2 instance has an unprotected port that is being probed by a known malicious host. **

This finding informs you that a port on an EC2 instance in your AWS environment is not blocked by a security group, access control list (ACL), or an on-host firewall (for example, Linux IPChains), and known scanners on the internet are actively probing it. If the identified unprotected port is 22 or 3389 and you often connect to this EC2 instance by using SSH/RDP and therefore can't block access to either of these ports, you can still limit exposure by allowing access to these ports only to the IP addresses from your corporate network IP address space. To restrict access to port 22 on Linux, see http://docs.aws.amazon.com/AWSEC2/

latest/UserGuide/authorizing-access-to-an-instance.html. To restrict access to port 3389 on Windows, see http://docs.aws.amazon.com/AWSEC2/latest/WindowsGuide/authorizing-access-to-an-instance.html.

For more information, see Remediating a Compromised EC2 Instance.

Recon:IAMUser/TorIPCaller

Finding description

**An API was invoked from a Tor exit node IP address. **

This finding informs you that an API operation that can list or describe your AWS resources was invoked from a Tor exit node IP address. Tor is software for enabling anonymous communication. It encrypts and randomly bounces communications through relays between a series of network nodes. The last Tor node is called the exit node. This can be a reconnaissance attack: an anonymous user trying to gather information or gain access to your AWS resources for malicious purposes. For more information, see Remediating Compromised AWS Credentials.

Recon:IAMUser/MaliciousIPCaller.Custom

Finding description

An API was invoked from an IP address on a custom threat list.

This finding informs you that an API operation that can list or describe your AWS resources was invoked from an IP address that is included on a threat list that you uploaded. In GuardDuty, a threat list consists of known malicious IP addresses. GuardDuty generates findings based on uploaded threat lists. This can be a reconnaissance attack: an anonymous user trying to gather information or gain access to your AWS resources for malicious purposes. For more information, see Remediating Compromised AWS Credentials.

Recon:IAMUser/MaliciousIPCaller

Finding description

An API was invoked from a known malicious IP address.

This finding informs you that an API operation that can list or describe your AWS resources was invoked from an IP address that is included on a threat list. In GuardDuty, a threat list consists of known malicious IP addresses. GuardDuty generates findings based on the custom or internal threat lists. This can be a reconnaissance attack: an anonymous user trying to gather information or gain access to your AWS resources for malicious purposes. For more information, see Remediating Compromised AWS Credentials.

Recon:EC2/Portscan

Finding description

EC2 instance is performing outbound port scans to a remote host.

This finding informs you that there is an EC2 instance in your AWS environment that is engaged in a possible port scan attack because it is trying to connect to multiple ports over a short period of time. The purpose of a port scan attack is to locate open ports to discover what services the machine is running and to identify its operating system. Your EC2 instance might be compromised. For more information, see Remediating a Compromised EC2 Instance.

Recon:IAMUser/NetworkPermissions

Finding description

An IAM user invoked an API commonly used to discover the network access permissions of existing security groups, ACLs, and routes in your AWS account.

This finding informs you that a specific IAM user in your AWS environment is exhibiting behavior that is different from the established baseline. This IAM user has no prior history of invoking this API. Your credentials might be compromised. For more information, see Remediating Compromised AWS Credentials.

This finding is triggered when network configuration settings in your AWS environment are probed under suspicious circumstances. For example, if an IAM user in your AWS environment with no prior history of doing so, invoked the DescribeSecurityGroups API. An attacker might use stolen credentials to perform this reconnaissance of network configuration settings before executing the next stage of their attack by changing network permissions or making use of existing openings in the network configuration.

Recon:IAMUser/ResourcePermissions

Finding description

An IAM user invoked an API commonly used to discover the permissions associated with various resources in your AWS account.

This finding informs you that a specific IAM user in your AWS environment is exhibiting behavior that is different from the established baseline. This IAM user has no prior history of invoking this API. Your credentials might be compromised. For more information, see Remediating Compromised AWS Credentials.

This finding is triggered when resource access permissions in your AWS account are probed under suspicious circumstances. For example, if an IAM user with no prior history of doing so, invoked the DescribeInstances API. An attacker might use stolen credentials to perform this reconnaissance of your AWS resources in order to find valuable information or determine the capabilities of the credentials they already have.

Recon:IAMUser/UserPermissions

Finding description

An IAM user invoked an API commonly used to discover the users, groups, policies and permissions in your AWS account.

This finding informs you that a specific IAM user in your AWS environment is exhibiting behavior that is different from the established baseline. This IAM user has no prior history of invoking this API. Your credentials might be compromised. For more information, see Remediating Compromised AWS Credentials.

This finding is triggered when user permissions in your AWS environment are probed under suspicious circumstances. For example, if an IAM user with no prior history of doing so, invoked the ListInstanceProfilesForRole API. An attacker might use stolen credentials to perform this reconnaissance of your IAM users and roles in order to determine the capabilities of the credentials they already have or to find more permissive credentials that are vulnerable to lateral movement.

ResourceConsumption:IAMUser/ComputeResources

Finding description

An IAM user invoked an API commonly used to launch compute resources like EC2 Instances.

This finding informs you that a specific IAM user in your AWS environment is exhibiting behavior that is different from the established baseline. This IAM user has no prior history of invoking this API. Your credentials might be compromised. For more information, see Remediating Compromised AWS Credentials.

This finding is triggered when EC2 instances in your AWS environment are launched under suspicious circumstances. For example, if an IAM user with no prior history of doing so, invoked the RunInstances API. This might be an indication of an attacker using stolen credentials to steal compute time (possibly for cryptocurrency mining or password cracking). It can also be an indication of an attacker using an EC2 instance in your AWS environment and its credentials to maintain access to your account.

Stealth:IAMUser/PasswordPolicyChange

Finding description

Account password policy was weakened.

Your AWS account password policy was weakened. For example, it was deleted or updated to require fewer characters, not require symbols and numbers, or required to extend the password expiration period. This finding can also be triggered by an attempt to update or delete your AWS account password policy. The AWS account password policy defines the rules that govern what kinds of passwords can be set for your IAM users. A weaker password policy permits the creation of passwords that are easy to remember and potentially easier to guess, thereby creating a security risk. For more information, see Remediating Compromised AWS Credentials.

Stealth:IAMUser/CloudTrailLoggingDisabled

Finding description

AWS CloudTrail trail was disabled.

This finding informs you that a CloudTrail trail within your AWS environment was disabled. This can be an attacker's attempt to disable logging to cover their tracks by eliminating any trace of their activity while gaining access to your AWS resources for malicious purposes. This finding can be triggered by a successful deletion or update of a trail. This finding can also be triggered by a successful deletion of an S3 bucket that stores the logs from a trail that is associated with GuardDuty. For more information, see Remediating Compromised AWS Credentials.

Stealth:IAMUser/LoggingConfigurationModified

Finding description

An IAM user invoked an API commonly used to stop CloudTrail logging, delete existing logs, and otherwise eliminate traces of activity in your AWS account.

This finding informs you that a specific IAM user in your AWS environment is exhibiting behavior that is different from the established baseline. This IAM user has no prior history of invoking this API. Your credentials might be compromised. For more information, see Remediating Compromised AWS Credentials.

This finding is triggered when the logging configuration in your AWS account is modified under suspicious circumstances. For example, if an IAM user with no prior history of doing so, invoked the StopLogging API. This can be an indication of an attacker trying to cover their tracks by eliminating any trace of their activity.

Trojan:EC2/BlackholeTraffic

Finding description

EC2 instance is attempting to communicate with an IP address of a remote host that is a known black hole.

This finding informs you that an EC2 instance in your AWS environment might be compromised because it is trying to communicate with an IP address of a black hole (or sink hole). Black holes refer to places in the network where incoming or outgoing traffic is silently discarded without informing the source that the data didn't reach its intended recipient. A black hole IP address specifies a host machine that is not running or an address to which no host has been assigned. For more information, see Remediating a Compromised EC2 Instance.

Trojan:EC2/DropPoint

Finding description

An EC2 instance is attempting to communicate with an IP address of a remote host that is known to hold credentials and other stolen data captured by malware.

This finding informs you that an EC2 instance in your AWS environment is trying communicate with an IP address of a remote host that is known to hold credentials and other stolen data captured by malware. Your EC2 instance might be compromised. For more information, see Remediating a Compromised EC2 Instance.

Trojan:EC2/BlackholeTraffic!DNS

Finding description

EC2 instance is querying a domain name that is being redirected to a black hole IP address.

This finding informs you that an EC2 instance in your AWS environment might be compromised because it is querying a domain name that is being redirected to a black hole IP address. Black holes refer to places in the network where incoming or outgoing traffic is silently discarded without informing the source that the data didn't reach its intended recipient. For more information, see Remediating a Compromised EC2 Instance.

Trojan:EC2/DriveBySourceTraffic!DNS

Finding description

EC2 instance is querying a domain name of a remote host that is a known source of Drive-By download attacks.

This finding informs you that an EC2 instance in your AWS environment might be compromised because it is querying a domain name of a remote host that is a known source of Drive-By download attacks. These are unintended downloads of computer software from the internet that can trigger an automatic install of a virus, spyware, or malware. For more information, see Remediating a Compromised EC2 Instance.

Trojan:EC2/DropPoint!DNS

Finding description

An EC2 instance is querying a domain name of a remote host that is known to hold credentials and other stolen data captured by malware.

This finding informs you that an EC2 instance in your AWS environment is querying a domain name of a remote host that is known to hold credentials and other stolen data captured by malware. Your EC2 instance might be compromised. For more information, see Remediating a Compromised EC2 Instance.

Trojan:EC2/DGADomainRequest.B

Finding description

EC2 instance is querying algorithmically generated domains. Such domains are commonly used by malware and could be an indication of a compromised EC2 instance.

This finding informs you that there is an EC2 instance in your AWS environment that is trying to query domain generation algorithms (DGA) domains. Your EC2 instance might be compromised.

Note
This finding is based on analysis of domain names using advanced heuristics, and hence may identify new DGA domains that are not present in Threat Intelligence feeds.

DGAs are used to periodically generate a large number of domain names that can be used as rendezvous points with their command and control (C&C) servers. C&C servers are computers that issue commands to members of a botnet, which is a collection of internet-connected devices that are infected and controlled by a common type of malware. The large number of potential rendezvous points makes it difficult to effectively shut down botnets because infected computers attempt to contact some of these domain names every day to receive updates or commands. For more information, see Remediating a Compromised EC2 Instance.

Trojan:EC2/DGADomainRequest.C!DNS

Finding description

EC2 instance is querying algorithmically generated domains. Such domains are commonly used by malware and could be an indication of a compromised EC2 instance.

This finding informs you that there is an EC2 instance in your AWS environment that is trying to query domain generation algorithms (DGA) domains. Your EC2 instance might be compromised.

Note
This finding is based on "known" DGA domains from GuardDuty's threat intelligence feeds.

DGAs are used to periodically generate a large number of domain names that can be used as rendezvous points with their command and control (C&C) servers. C&C servers are computers that issue commands to members of a botnet, which is a collection of internet-connected devices that are infected and controlled by a common type of malware. The large number of potential rendezvous points makes it difficult to effectively shut down botnets because infected computers attempt to contact some of these domain names every day to receive updates or commands. For more information, see Remediating a Compromised EC2 Instance.

Trojan:EC2/DNSDataExfiltration

Finding description

EC2 instance is exfiltrating data through DNS queries.

This finding informs you that there is an EC2 instance in your AWS environment with malware that uses DNS queries for outbound data transfers. The result is the exfiltration of data. Your EC2 instance might be compromised. DNS traffic is not typically blocked by firewalls. For example, malware in a compromised EC2 instance can encode data, (such as your credit card number), into a DNS query and send it to a remote DNS server that is controlled by an attacker. For more information, see Remediating a Compromised EC2 Instance.

Trojan:EC2/PhishingDomainRequest!DNS

Finding description

EC2 instance is querying domains involved in phishing attacks. Your EC2 instance might be compromised.

This finding informs you that there is an EC2 instance in your AWS environment that is trying to query a domain involved in phishing attacks. Phishing domains are set up by someone posing as a legitimate institution in order to induce individuals into providing sensitive data such as personally identifiable information, banking and credit card details, and passwords. Your EC2 instance is potentially trying to retrieve sensitive data stored on a phishing website. Or your EC2 instance is attempting to setup a phishing website. Your EC2 instance might be compromised. For more information, see Remediating a Compromised EC2 Instance.

UnauthorizedAccess:IAMUser/TorIPCaller

Finding description

An API was invoked from a Tor exit node IP address.

This finding informs you that an API operation (for example, an attempt to launch an EC2 instance, create a new IAM user, or modify your AWS privileges) was invoked from a Tor exit node IP address. Tor is software for enabling anonymous communication. It encrypts and randomly bounces communications through relays between a series of network nodes. The last Tor node is called the exit node. This can indicate unauthorized access to your AWS resources with the intent of hiding the attacker's true identity. For more information, see Remediating Compromised AWS Credentials.

UnauthorizedAccess:IAMUser/MaliciousIPCaller.Custom

Finding description

An API was invoked from an IP address on a custom threat list.

This finding informs you that an API operation (for example, an attempt to launch an EC2 instance, create a new IAM user, modify your AWS privileges, and so on) was invoked from an IP address that is included on a threat list that you uploaded. In GuardDuty, a threat list consists of known malicious IP addresses. GuardDuty generates findings based on uploaded threat lists. This can indicate unauthorized access to your AWS resources with the intent of hiding the attacker's true identity. For more information, see Remediating Compromised AWS Credentials.

UnauthorizedAccess:IAMUser/ConsoleLoginSuccess.B

Finding description

Multiple worldwide successful console logins were observed.

This finding informs you that multiple successful console logins for the same IAM user were observed around the same time in various geographical locations. Such anomalous and risky access location pattern indicates potential unauthorized access to your AWS resources. For more information, see Remediating Compromised AWS Credentials.

Note
This finding is only triggered by the activity of the following IAM identities: root, IAM users, and federated users. This finding is NOT triggered by the activity of an assumed role. For more information about IAM identities, see CloudTrail userIdentity Element.

UnauthorizedAccess:IAMUser/MaliciousIPCaller

Finding description

An API was invoked from a known malicious IP address.

This finding informs you that an API operation (for example, an attempt to launch an EC2 instance, create a new IAM user, modify your AWS privileges, and so on) was invoked from a known malicious IP address. This can indicate unauthorized access to your AWS resources. For more information, see Remediating Compromised AWS Credentials.

UnauthorizedAccess:IAMUser/UnusualASNCaller

Finding description

An API was invoked from an IP address of an unusual ISP.

This finding informs you that certain activity was invoked from an IP address of an unusual ISP. This ISP was never observed throughout your AWS usage history. This activity can include a console login, an attempt to launch an EC2 instance, create a new IAM user, modify your AWS privileges, etc. This can indicate unauthorized access to your AWS resources. For more information, see Remediating Compromised AWS Credentials.

UnauthorizedAccess:EC2/TorIPCaller

Finding description

EC2 instance is receiving inbound connections from a Tor exit node.

This finding informs you that an EC2 instance in your AWS environment is receiving inbound connections from a Tor exit node. Tor is software for enabling anonymous communication. It encrypts and randomly bounces communications through relays between a series of network nodes. This can indicate unauthorized access to your AWS resources with the intent of hiding the attacker's true identity. For more information, see Remediating a Compromised EC2 Instance.

UnauthorizedAccess:EC2/MaliciousIPCaller.Custom

Finding description

EC2 instance is communicating outbound with a IP address on a custom threat list.

This finding informs you that an EC2 instance in your AWS environment is communicating outbound using the TCP protocol with an IP address included on a threat list that you uploaded. In GuardDuty, a threat list consists of known malicious IP addresses. GuardDuty generates findings based on uploaded threat lists. This can indicate unauthorized access to your AWS resources. For more information, see Remediating a Compromised EC2 Instance.

UnauthorizedAccess:EC2/SSHBruteForce

Finding description

EC2 instance has been involved in SSH brute force attacks.

This finding informs you that an EC2 instance in your AWS environment was involved in a brute force attack aimed at obtaining passwords to SSH services on Linux-based systems. This can indicate unauthorized access to your AWS resources.

Note
This finding is generated only through GuardDuty monitoring traffic on port 22. If your SSH services are configured to use other ports, this finding is not generated.

For more information, see Remediating a Compromised EC2 Instance.

UnauthorizedAccess:EC2/RDPBruteForce

Finding description

EC2 instance has been involved in RDP brute force attacks.

This finding informs you that an EC2 instance in your AWS environment was involved in a brute force attack aimed at obtaining passwords to RDP services on Windows-based systems. This can indicate unauthorized access to your AWS resources. For more information, see Remediating a Compromised EC2 Instance.

UnauthorizedAccess:IAMUser/InstanceCredentialExfiltration

Finding description

Credentials that were created exclusively for an EC2 instance through an instance launch role are being used from an external IP address.

This finding informs you of attempts to run AWS API operations from a host outside of EC2, using temporary AWS credentials that were created on an EC2 instance in your AWS account. Your EC2 instance might be compromised, and the temporary credentials from this instance might have been exfiltrated to a remote host outside of AWS. AWS does not recommend redistributing temporary credentials outside of the entity that created them (for example, AWS applications, EC2, or Lambda). However, authorized users can export credentials from their EC2 instances to make legitimate API calls. To rule out a potential attack and verify the legitimacy of the activity, contact the IAM user to whom these credentials are assigned. For more information, see Remediating Compromised AWS Credentials.

This finding is commonly triggered in AWS Direct Connect scenarios where all traffic from EC2 instances is routed into your on-premises network and out your own firewall, thus appearing to originate from an IP address that is external to EC2. If it's common practice in your AWS production environment to exfiltrate temporary AWS credentials created on EC2 instances, you can whitelist this finding by adding the IP address listed in the **service.action.awsApiCallAction.remoteIpDetails.ipAddressV4** field in the finding's JSON to your active trusted IP list. (You can view the finding's complete JSON, by selecting the finding in the console, and then choosing **Actions/Export**, or by running the GetFindings API operation). A GuardDuty trusted IP list consists of IP addresses that you have whitelisted for secure communication with your AWS infrastructure and applications. GuardDuty does not generate findings for IP addresses on trusted IP lists. For more information, see Working with Trusted IP Lists and Threat Lists

UnauthorizedAccess:IAMUser/ConsoleLogin

Finding description

**An unusual console login by an IAM user in your AWS account was observed. **

This finding informs you that a specific IAM user in your AWS environment is exhibiting behavior that is different from the established baseline. This IAM user has no prior history of login activity using this client application from this specific location. Your IAM user credentials might be compromised. For more information, see Remediating Compromised AWS Credentials.

This finding is triggered when a console login is detected under suspicious circumstances. For example, if an IAM user with no prior history of doing so, invoked the ConsoleLogin API from a never-before-used client or an unusual location. This could be an indication of stolen credentials being used to gain access to your AWS account, or a valid user accessing the account in an invalid or less secure manner (for example, not over an approved VPN).

Complete List of GuardDuty Retired Finding Types

The following are finding types that have been retired (no longer generated) in GuardDuty:

Important
You cannot reactivate retired GuardDuty findings types.

Topics

- Behavior:IAMUser/InstanceLaunchUnusual
- CryptoCurrency:EC2/BitcoinTool.A

Behavior:IAMUser/InstanceLaunchUnusual

Finding description

An IAM user launched an EC2 instance of an unusual type.

This finding informs you that a specific IAM user in your AWS environment is exhibiting behavior that is different from the established baseline. This IAM user has no prior history of launching an EC2 instance of this type. Your IAM user credentials might be compromised. For more information, see Remediating Compromised AWS Credentials

CryptoCurrency:EC2/BitcoinTool.A

Finding description

EC2 instance is communicating with Bitcoin mining pools.

This finding informs you that an EC2 instance in your AWS environment is communicating with Bitcoin mining pools. In the field of cryptocurrency mining, a mining pool is the pooling of resources by miners who share their processing power over a network to split the reward according to the amount of work they contributed to solving a block. Unless you use this EC2 instance for Bitcoin mining, your EC2 instance might be compromised. For more information, see Remediating a Compromised EC2 Instance.

Remediating Security Issues Discovered by Amazon GuardDuty

Amazon GuardDuty generates findings that indicate potential security issues. In this release of GuardDuty, the potential security issues indicate either a compromised EC2 instance or a set of compromised credentials in your AWS environment. The following sections describe the recommended remediation steps for either scenario.

Topics

- Remediating a Compromised EC2 Instance
- Remediating Compromised AWS Credentials

Remediating a Compromised EC2 Instance

Follow these recommended steps to remediate a compromised EC2 instance in your AWS environment:

- Investigate the potentially compromised instance for malware and remove any discovered malware. You can also refer to the AWS Marketplace for partner products that might help to identify and remove malware.
- If you are unable to identify and stop unauthorized activity on your EC2 instance, we recommend that you terminate the compromised EC2 instance and replace it with a new instance as needed. The following are additional resources for securing your EC2 instances:
    - "Security and Network" section in Best Practices for Amazon EC2.
    - Amazon EC2 Security Groups for Linux Instances and Amazon EC2 Security Groups for Windows Instances.
    - Tips for securing your EC2 instances (Linux) and Securing Windows EC2 Instances.
    - AWS Security Best Practices
- Browse for further assistance on the AWS developer forums: https://forums.aws.amazon.com/index.jspa
- If you are a Premium Support package subscriber, you can request one-one-one assistance.

Remediating Compromised AWS Credentials

Follow these recommended steps to remediate compromised credentials in your AWS environment:

- **Identify the owner of the credentials.**

    If a GuardDuty finding informs you of a potential compromise to AWS credentials, you can locate the affected IAM user by their access keys or user name. **Note**
    Users need their own access keys to make programmatic calls to AWS from the AWS Command Line Interface (AWS CLI), Tools for Windows PowerShell, the AWS SDKs, or direct HTTP calls using the APIs for individual AWS services. To fill this need, you can create, modify, view, or rotate access keys (access key IDs and secret access keys) for IAM users. For more information, see Managing Access Keys for IAM Users.

    To find the access key ID or user name that belongs to a potentially compromised IAM user, open the console and view the details pane of the finding that you're analyzing. For more information, see Locating and Analyzing GuardDuty Findings. After you have the access key ID or user name, open the IAM console, choose the **Users** tab, and locate the affected user by typing the access key ID or user name in the **Find users by username or access key** search field.

- **Determine whether the credentials were used by the IAM user legitimately.**

    Contact the IAM user that you've located, and verify whether the user legitimately used the access key and user name that is identified in the GuardDuty finding. For example, find out if the user did the following:

    - Invoked the API operation that was listed in the GuardDuty finding
    - Invoked the API operation at the time that is listed in the GuardDuty finding
    - Invoked the API operation from the IP address that is listed in the GuardDuty finding

If you confirm that the activity is a legitimate use of the AWS credentials, you can ignore the GuardDuty finding. If not, this activity is likely the result of a compromise to that particular access key, the IAM user's user ID and password, or possibly the entire AWS account. You can then use the information in the My AWS account may be compromised article to remediate the issue.

Working with Trusted IP Lists and Threat Lists

Amazon GuardDuty monitors the security of your AWS environment by analyzing and processing VPC Flow Logs, AWS CloudTrail event logs, and DNS logs. You can expand this monitoring scope by configuring GuardDuty to also use your own custom *trusted IP lists* and *threat lists*.

Trusted IP lists consist of IP addresses that you have whitelisted for secure communication with your AWS infrastructure and applications. GuardDuty does not generate findings for IP addresses on trusted IP lists. At any given time, you can have only one uploaded trusted IP list per AWS account per region.

Threat lists consist of known malicious IP addresses. GuardDuty generates findings based on threat lists. At any given time, you can have up to six uploaded threat lists per AWS account per region.

Users from master GuardDuty accounts can upload and manage trusted IP lists and threat lists. Users from member GuardDuty accounts CANNOT upload and manage lists. Trusted IP lists and threat lists that are uploaded by the master account are imposed on GuardDuty functionality in its member accounts. In other words, in member accounts GuardDuty generates findings based on activity that involves known malicious IP addresses from the master's threat lists and does not generate findings based on activity that involves IP addresses from the master's trusted IP lists. For more information, see Managing AWS Accounts in Amazon GuardDuty.

Important
GuardDuty uses the same `AWSServiceRoleForAmazonGuardDuty` service-linked role that is automatically assigned to it when you enable GuardDuty for the permissions required to evaluate your trusted IP lists and threat lists.

Note the following when creating trusted IP lists and threat lists that you plan to upload with GuardDuty:

- In your trusted IP lists and threat lists, IP addresses and CIDR ranges must appear one per line.

  The following is a sample list in Plaintext format:

```
1 54.20.175.217
2 205.0.0.0/8
```

- GuardDuty doesn't generate findings for any non-routable or internal IP addresses in your threat lists.

- GuardDuty doesn't generate findings based on activity that involves domain names that are included in your threat lists. GuardDuty only generates findings based on activity that involves IP addresses and CIDR ranges in your threat lists.

Topics
- Permissions Required to Upload Trusted IP Lists and Threat Lists
- To Upload Trusted IP Lists and Threat Lists
- To Activate or Deactivate Trusted IP Lists and Threat Lists
- To Update Trusted IP Lists and Threat Lists

Permissions Required to Upload Trusted IP Lists and Threat Lists

Various IAM identity require proper permissions to work with trusted IP lists and threat lists in GuardDuty. An identity with the **AmazonGuardDutyFullAccess** managed policy attached can only rename and deactivate uploaded trusted IP lists and threat lists.

To grant various identities full access to working with trusted IP lists and threat lists (in addition to renaming and deactivating, this includes uploading, activating, deleting, and updating the location of the lists), make sure that the following actions are present in the permissions policy attached to an IAM user, group, or role:

```
1      {
2          "Effect": "Allow",
3          "Action": [
4              "iam:PutRolePolicy",
```

```
5            "iam:DeleteRolePolicy"
6        ],
7        "Resource": "arn:aws:iam::123456789123:role/aws-service-role/guardduty.amazonaws.com
             /AWSServiceRoleForAmazonGuardDuty"
8    }
```

Important

These actions are not included in the **AmazonGuardDutyFullAccess** managed policy.

To Upload Trusted IP Lists and Threat Lists

The following procedure describes how you can upload trusted IP lists and threat lists using the GuardDuty console.

To upload trusted IP lists and threat lists (console)

1. Open the GuardDuty console at https://console.aws.amazon.com/guardduty.

2. In the navigation pane, under **Settings**, choose **Lists**.

3. On the **List management** page, choose **Add a trusted IP list** or **Add a threat list**.

4. In the dialog box, do the following:

   - For **List name**, type a name for the list.
   - For **Location**, specify the location of the list - this is the S3 bucket where you store your trusted IP list or threat list and the file that contains your list. **Note**
     You can specify the location URL in the following formats:
     https://s3/.amazonaws/.com/bucket/.name/file/.txt https://s3/-aws/-region/.amazonaws/.com/ bucket/.name/file/.txt http://bucket/.s3/.amazonaws/.com/file/.txt http://bucket/.s3/-aws/-region/ .amazonaws/.com/file/.txt s3://mybucket/file.txt
   - For **Format**, choose your list's file type.
   - Select the **I agree** check box.
   - Choose **Add list**.

To Activate or Deactivate Trusted IP Lists and Threat Lists

The following procedures describe how you can activate or deactivate trusted IP lists and threat lists in GuardDuty once they are uploaded. GuardDuty includes the uploaded lists in its monitoring of your AWS environment only if they are active.

To activate trusted IP lists and threat lists (console)

1. Open the GuardDuty console at https://console.aws.amazon.com/guardduty.

2. In the navigation pane, under **Settings**, choose **Lists**.

3. On the **List management** page, locate the trusted IP set or a threat list that you want to activate, and then choose the radio button under the **Active** column.

To deactivate trusted IP lists and threat lists (API or CLI)

- Currently in GuardDuty, deactivating trusted IP lists and threat lists through the console is not supported.

  You can deactivate your trusted IP lists or threat lists by running the UpdateIPSet and UpdateThreatIntelSet APIs or the update-ip-set and update-threat-intel-set CLI commands.

  For example, you can run the following command:

```
1 aws guardduty update-ip-set --detector-id <detector-id> --ip-set-id <ip-set-id> --no-
    activate
```

Make sure to replace <detector-id> and <ip-set-id> with a valid detector ID and trusted IP list ID.

To Update Trusted IP Lists and Threat Lists

If you make changes to a trusted IP list or a threat list that is already uploaded and activated in GuardDuty (for example, rename the list or add more IP addresses to it), you must update this list in GuardDuty and reactivate it in order for GuardDuty to use the latest version of the list in its security monitoring scope. To update a safe or threat list, you can either use the procedure below or run the UpdateIPSet or UpdateThreatIntelSet APIs.

To update trusted IP lists and threat lists (console)

1. Open the GuardDuty console at https://console.aws.amazon.com/guardduty.

2. In the navigation pane, under **Settings**, choose **Lists**.

3. On the **List management** page, locate the trusted IP set or a threat list that you want to update, and then choose the pencil icon under the **Active** column.

4. In the **Update list** pop up window, verify all specified list information, choose **I agree**, and then choose **Update list**.

5. On the **List management** page, locate the trusted IP set or a threat list that you want to activate again, and then choose the radio button under the **Active** column.

Managing AWS Accounts in Amazon GuardDuty

You can invite other accounts to enable GuardDuty and become associated with your AWS account. If your invitations are accepted, your account is designated as the **master** GuardDuty account, and the associated accounts become your **member** accounts. You can then view and manage their GuardDuty findings on their behalf. In GuardDuty, a master account (per region) can have up to 1000 member accounts.

An AWS account cannot be a GuardDuty master and member account at the same time. An AWS account can accept only one GuardDuty membership invitation. Accepting a membership invitation is optional.

The sections below describe how you can create master and member accounts using the GuardDuty console, CLI, and APIs. You can also create master and member accounts through AWS CloudFormation. For more information, see AWS::GuardDuty::Master and AWS::GuardDuty::Member.

Note
Cross-regional data transfer can occur when GuardDuty member accounts are created. In order to verify member accounts' email addresses, GuardDuty uses a non-AWS account information verification service that operates only in the AWS US East (N. Virginia) region.

Topics

- GuardDuty Master Accounts
- GuardDuty Member Accounts
- Designating Master and Member Accounts Through GuardDuty Console
- Designating Master and Member Accounts Through the GuardDuty API Operations
- Enable GuardDuty in Multiple Accounts Simultaneously

GuardDuty Master Accounts

Users from the master account can configure GuardDuty as well as view and manage GuardDuty findings for their own account and all of their member accounts.

The following is how users from a master account can configure GuardDuty:

- Users from a master account can generate sample findings in their own account. Users from a master account CANNOT generate sample findings in members' accounts.
- Users from a master account can archive findings in their own accounts and in all member accounts.
- Users from a master account can upload and further manage trusted IP lists and threat lists in their own account. **Important**
  Trusted IP lists and threat lists that are uploaded by the master account and in the master account are imposed on GuardDuty functionality in its member accounts. In other words, in member accounts GuardDuty generates findings based on activity that involves known malicious IP addresses from the master's threat lists and does not generate findings based on activity that involves IP addresses from the master's trusted IP lists.
- Users from a master account can suspend GuardDuty for its own (master) account. Users from a master account can also suspend GuardDuty in its member accounts. **Note**
  If a master account user suspends GuardDuty in the master account, this suspension is NOT automatically imposed on the member accounts. To suspend GuardDuty for member accounts, a user from a master account must select these member accounts and suspend GuardDuty through the console or specify their account IDs when running the StopMonitoringMembers API.
  A master account user can also re-enable GuardDuty in member accounts either through the console or by running the StartMonitoringMembers API.
- Users from a master account can disable GuardDuty in its own (master) account. However, all member accounts must first be removed to disable GuardDuty in the master account. Users from a master account CANNOT disable GuardDuty for member accounts.

GuardDuty Member Accounts

Users from member accounts can configure GuardDuty as well as view and manage GuardDuty findings in their account. Member account users CANNOT configure GuardDuty or view or manage findings in the master or other member accounts.

The following is how users from a member account can configure GuardDuty:

- Users from a member account can generate sample findings in their own member account. Users from a member account CANNOT generate sample findings in the master or other member accounts.

- Users from a member account CANNOT archive findings either in their own account or in their master's account, or in other member accounts.

- Users from a member account CANNOT upload and further manage trusted IP lists and threat lists.

  Trusted IP lists and threat lists that are uploaded by the master account are imposed on GuardDuty functionality in its member accounts. In other words, in member accounts GuardDuty generates findings based on activity that involves known malicious IP addresses from the master's threat lists and does not generate findings based on activity that involves IP addresses from the master's trusted IP lists. **Note** When a GuardDuty account becomes a GuardDuty member account, all of its trusted IP lists and threat lists (uploaded prior to becoming a GuardDuty member account) are disabled. If a GuardDuty member account disassociates from its GuardDuty master account, all of its trusted IP lists and threat lists (uploaded prior to becoming a GuardDuty member account) are re-enabled. Once no longer a GuardDuty member account, this account's users can upload and further manage trusted IP lists and threat lists in this account.

- Users from a member account can suspend GuardDuty for their own account. Users from a member account CANNOT suspend GuardDuty for the master account or other member accounts.

- Users from member accounts can disable GuardDuty for their own account. Users from a member account CANNOT disable GuardDuty for the master account or other member accounts.

Designating Master and Member Accounts Through GuardDuty Console

In GuardDuty, your account is designated a master account when you add another AWS account to be associated with your account or when another account accepts your invitation to become a member account.

If your account is a non-master account, you can accept an invitation from another account. When you accept, your account becomes a member account.

Use the following procedures to add an account, invite an account, or accept an invitation from another account.

- Step 1 - Add an account
- Step 2 - Invite an account
- Step 3 - Accept an invitation

Step 1 - Add an account

1. Open the GuardDuty console at https://console.aws.amazon.com/guardduty.

2. In the navigation pane, under **Settings**, choose **Accounts**.

3. Choose **Add accounts**.

4. On the **Add member** accounts page, under **Enter accounts**, type the AWS account ID and email address of the account that you want to add. Then choose **Add account**.

   You can add more accounts, one at a time, by specifying their IDs and email addresses. You can also choose **Upload list (.csv)** to bulk add accounts. This can be useful if you want to invite some of these accounts to enable GuardDuty right away but want to delay for others. **Important**
   In your .csv list, accounts must appear one per line. For each account in your .csv list, you must specify

the account ID and the email address separated by a comma. The first line of your .csv file must contain the following header, as shown in the example below: **Account ID,Email**. Each subsequent line must contain a valid account ID and a valid email address for the account that you want to add. The account ID and email address must be separated by a comma.

```
1 Account ID,Email
2 111111111111,user@example.com
```

5. When you are finished adding accounts, choose **Done**.

The added accounts appear in a list on the **Accounts** page. Each added account in this list has an **Invite** link in the **Status** column.

Step 2 - Invite an account

1. Open the GuardDuty console at https://console.aws.amazon.com/guardduty.

2. In the navigation pane, under **Settings**, choose **Accounts**.

3. For the account that you want to invite to enable GuardDuty, choose the **Invite** link that appears in the **Status** column of the added accounts list.

4. In the **Invitation to GuardDuty** dialog box, type an invitation message (optional), and then choose **Send notification**.

The value in the **Status** column for the invited account changes to **Pending**.

Step 3 - Accept an invitation

1. Open the GuardDuty console at https://console.aws.amazon.com/guardduty.

2. Do one of the following:

   - If you don't have GuardDuty enabled, on the **Enable GuardDuty** page, choose **Enable GuardDuty**. Then use the **Accept** widget and the **Accept invitation** button to accept the membership invitation. **Important**
     You must enable GuardDuty before you can accept a membership invitation.
   - If you already have GuardDuty enabled, use the **Accept** widget and the **Accept invitation** button to accept the membership invitation.

After you accept the invitation, your account becomes a GuardDuty member account. The account whose user sent the invitation becomes the GuardDuty master account. The master account user can see that the value in the **Status** column for your member account changes to **Monitored**. The master account user can now view and manage GuardDuty findings for your member account.

Designating Master and Member Accounts Through the GuardDuty API Operations

You can also designate master and member GuardDuty accounts through the API operations. The following is the order in which these particular GuardDuty API operations must be run in order to designate master and member accounts in GuardDuty.

Complete the following procedure using the credentials of the AWS account that you want to designate as the GuardDuty master account.

---

1. Run the CreateMembers API operation using the credentials of the AWS account that has GuardDuty enabled (this is the account that you want to be the master GuardDuty account).

You must specify the detector ID of the current AWS account and the account details (account ID and email address) of the account(s) of the accounts that you want to become GuardDuty members (you can create one or more members with this API operation).

You can also do this by using AWS Command Line Tools. You can run the following CLI command (make sure to use your own valid detector ID, account ID, and email:

```
1 aws guardduty create-members --detector-id 12abc34d567e8fa901bc2d34e56789f0 --account-
    details AccountId=123456789012,Email=guarddutymember@amazon.com
```

2. Run the InviteMembers API operation using the credentials of the AWS account that has GuardDuty enabled (this is the account that you want to be the master GuardDuty account.

You must specify the detector ID of the current AWS account and the account IDs (you can invite one or more members with this API operation) of the accounts that you want to become GuardDuty members.
Note
You can also specify an optional invitation message using the `message` request parameter.

You can also do this by using AWS Command Line Tools. You can run the following CLI command (make sure to use your own valid detector ID and account IDs:

```
1 aws guardduty invite-members --detector-id 12abc34d567e8fa901bc2d34e56789f0 --account-ids
    123456789012
```

Complete the following procedure using the credentials of each AWS account that you want to designate as the GuardDuty member account.

---

1. Run the CreateDetector API operation for each AWS account that was invited to become a GuardDuty member account and where you want to accept an invitation.

You must specify if the detector resource is to be enabled using the GuardDuty service. A detector must be created and enabled in order for GuardDuty to become operational. You must first enable GuardDuty before accepting an invitation.

You can also do this by using AWS Command Line Tools. You can run the following CLI command:

```
1 aws guardduty create-detector --enable
```

2. Run the AcceptInvitation API operation for each AWS account where you want to accept the membership invitation using that account's credentials.

You must specify the detector ID of this AWS account (member account), the master ID of the AWS account that sent the invitation that you are accepting (you can get this value either from the invitation email or by running the ListInvitations API operation. It is the value of the `accountID` response parameter), and the invitation ID of the invitation that you are accepting.

You can also do this by using AWS Command Line Tools. You can run the following CLI command (make sure to use valide detector ID, master account ID, and invitation ID:

```
1 aws guardduty accept-invitation --detector-id 12abc34d567e8fa901bc2d34e56789f0 --master-id
    012345678901 --invitation-id 84b097800250d17d1872b34c4daadcf5
```

Enable GuardDuty in Multiple Accounts Simultaneously

To enable GuardDuty in multiple accounts at the same time, you can run enableguardduty.py and disableguardduty.py, which you can download from the following page: https://github.com/aws-samples/amazon-guardduty-multiaccount-scripts.

enableguardduty.py enables GuardDuty, sends invitations from the master account and accepts invitations in all member accounts. The result is a master GuardDuty account that contains all security findings for all member accounts. Since GuardDuty is regionally isolated, findings for each member account roll up to the corresponding region in the master account. For example, the us-east-1 region in your GuardDuty master account contains the security findings for all us-east-1 findings from all associated member accounts.

The scripts are modelled with the StackSets service in mind and are therefore dependent on having the IAM role called **AWSCloudFormationStackSetExecutionRole** in each account where you want to enable GuardDuty. This role provides StackSets with access to GuardDuty. If you already use StackSets, the scripts can leverage your existing roles. If not, you can use the instructions in https://docs.aws.amazon.com/AWSCloudFormation/latest/UserGuide/stacksets-prereqs.html to setup the **AWSCloudFormationStackSetExecutionRole** in each account where you want to enable GuardDuty.

Launch a new Amazon Linux instance with a role that has administrative permissions. Login to this instance and run the following commands:

```
1 sudo yum install git python
2 sudo pip install boto3
3 aws configure
4 git clone https://github.com/aws-samples/amazon-guardduty-multiaccount-scripts.git
5 cd amazon-guardduty-multiaccount-scripts
6 sudo chmod +x disableguardduty.py enableguardduty.py
```

Note

When prompted, set the region to us-east-1 or whatever default region you want.

The scripts have one parameter - the account ID of your GuardDuty master account. Before you execute enableguardduty.py or disableguardduty.py, update either script's global variables to map to your AWS accounts. You can create a list of the accounts and their associated email addresses. Specify the master GuardDuty account and (optionally) customize the invite message that is sent to member accounts.

Suspending or Disabling Amazon GuardDuty

You can use the GuardDuty console to suspend or disable GuardDuty.

- If you suspend GuardDuty, it no longer monitors the security of your AWS environment or generates new findings. Your existing findings remain intact and are not affected by the GuardDuty suspension. You can choose to re-enable GuardDuty later. **Important**
  You are not charged for using GuardDuty when the service is suspended.
- If you disable GuardDuty, your existing findings and the GuardDuty configuration are lost and can't be recovered. If you want to save your existing findings, you must export them before you disable GuardDuty.

To suspend or disable GuardDuty (console)

1. Open the GuardDuty console at https://console.aws.amazon.com/guardduty.

2. In the navigation pane, under **Settings**, choose **General**.

3. Choose either **Suspend GuardDuty** or **Disable GuardDuty**. Then choose **Save settings**.

Logging Amazon GuardDuty API Calls with AWS CloudTrail

Amazon GuardDuty is integrated with AWS CloudTrail, a service that provides a record of actions taken by a user, role, or an AWS service in GuardDuty. CloudTrail captures API calls for GuardDuty as events, including calls from the GuardDuty console and from code calls to the GuardDuty APIs. If you create a trail, you can enable continuous delivery of CloudTrail events to an Amazon S3 bucket, including events for GuardDuty. If you don't configure a trail, you can still view the most recent events in the CloudTrail console in **Event history**. Using the information collected by CloudTrail, you can determine the request that was made to GuardDuty, the IP address the request was made from, who made the request, when it was made, and more.

To learn more about CloudTrail, including how to configure and enable it, see the *AWS CloudTrail User Guide.*

GuardDuty Information in CloudTrail

CloudTrail is enabled on your AWS account when you create the account. When supported event activity occurs in GuardDuty, that activity is recorded in a CloudTrail event along with other AWS service events in **Event history**. You can view, search, and download recent events in your AWS account. For more information, see Viewing Events with CloudTrail Event History.

For an ongoing record of events in your AWS account, including events for GuardDuty, create a trail. A trail enables CloudTrail to deliver log files to an Amazon S3 bucket. By default, when you create a trail in the console, the trail applies to all regions. The trail logs events from all regions in the AWS partition and delivers the log files to the Amazon S3 bucket that you specify. Additionally, you can configure other AWS services to further analyze and act upon the event data collected in CloudTrail logs. For more information, see:

- Overview for Creating a Trail
- CloudTrail Supported Services and Integrations
- Configuring Amazon SNS Notifications for CloudTrail
- Receiving CloudTrail Log Files from Multiple Regions and Receiving CloudTrail Log Files from Multiple Accounts

All GuardDuty actions are logged by CloudTrail and are documented in the Amazon GuardDuty API Reference.

Every event or log entry contains information about who generated the request. The identity information helps you determine the following:

- Whether the request was made with root or IAM user credentials
- Whether the request was made with temporary security credentials for a role or federated user
- Whether the request was made by another AWS service

For more information, see the CloudTrail userIdentity Element.

Example: GuardDuty Log File Entries

A trail is a configuration that enables delivery of events as log files to an Amazon S3 bucket that you specify. CloudTrail log files contain one or more log entries. An event represents a single request from any source and includes information about the requested action, the date and time of the action, request parameters, and so on. CloudTrail log files aren't an ordered stack trace of the public API calls, so they don't appear in any specific order.

The following example shows a CloudTrail log entry that demonstrates the `CreateIPThreatIntelSet` action.

```
1  {
2      "eventVersion": "1.05",
3      "userIdentity": {
4          "type": "AssumedRole",
5          "principalId": "AIDACKCEVSQ6C2EXAMPLE",
```

```
6       "arn": "arn:aws:iam::444455556666:user/Alice",
7       "accountId": "444455556666",
8       "accessKeyId": "AKIAI44QH8DHBEXAMPLE",
9       "sessionContext": {
10          "attributes": {
11              "mfaAuthenticated": "false",
12              "creationDate": "2018-06-14T22:54:20Z"
13          },
14          "sessionIssuer": {
15              "type": "Role",
16              "principalId": "AIDACKCEVSQ6C2EXAMPLE",
17              "arn": "arn:aws:iam::444455556666:user/Alice",
18              "accountId": "444455556666",
19              "userName": "Alice"
20          }
21      }
22  },
23  "eventTime": "2018-06-14T22:57:56Z",
24  "eventSource": "guardduty.amazonaws.com",
25  "eventName": "CreateThreatIntelSet",
26  "awsRegion": "us-west-2",
27  "sourceIPAddress": "54.240.230.177",
28  "userAgent": "console.amazonaws.com",
29  "requestParameters": {
30      "detectorId": "5ab04b1110c865eecf516eee2435ede7",
31      "name": "Example",
32      "format": "TXT",
33      "activate": false,
34      "location": "https://s3.amazonaws.com/bucket.name/file.txt"
35  },
36  "responseElements": {
37      "threatIntelSetId": "1ab200428351c99d859bf61992460d24"
38  },
39  "requestID": "5f6bf981-7026-11e8-a9fc-5b37d2684c5c",
40  "eventID": "81337b11-e5c8-4f91-b141-deb405625bc9",
41  "readOnly": false,
42  "eventType": "AwsApiCall",
43  "recipientAccountId": "444455556666"
44 }
```

From this event information, you can determine that the request was made to create a threat list Example in GuardDuty. You can also see that the request was made by an IAM user named Alice on June 14, 2018.

Monitoring Amazon GuardDuty Findings with Amazon CloudWatch Events

Amazon GuardDuty sends notifications based on Amazon CloudWatch Events when any change in the findings takes place. An event indicates a change in your AWS environment. In the context of GuardDuty, such changes include newly generated findings and all subsequent occurrences of these existing findings. All subsequent occurrences of an existing finding are always assigned a finding ID that is identical to the ID of the original finding.

Every GuardDuty finding is assigned a finding ID. GuardDuty creates a CloudWatch event for every finding with a unique finding ID. For a newly generated finding with a unique finding ID, GuardDuty sends a notification based on its CloudWatch event within 5 minutes of the finding. This event (and this notification) also includes all subsequent occurrences of this finding that take place in the first 5 minutes since this finding with a unique ID is generated.

For every finding with a unique finding ID, GuardDuty aggregates all subsequent occurrences of a particular finding that take place in six-hour intervals into a single event. GuardDuty then sends a notification about these subsequent occurrences based on this event. In other words, for the subsequent occurrences of the existing findings, GuardDuty sends notifications based on CloudWatch events every 6 hours.

The CloudWatch event for GuardDuty has the following format:

```
1      {
2        "version": "0",
3        "id": "cd2d702e-ab31-411b-9344-793ce56b1bc7",
4        "detail-type": "GuardDuty Finding",
5        "source": "aws.guardduty",
6        "account": "111122223333",
7        "time": "1970-01-01T00:00:00Z",
8        "region": "us-east-1",
9        "resources": [],
10       "detail": {COMPLETE_GUARDDUTY_FINDING_JSON}
11     }
```

For the complete list of all the parameters included in the COMPLETE_GUARDDUTY_FINDING_JSON, see Response Syntax. The id parameter that appears in the COMPLETE_GUARDDUTY_FINDING_JSON is the finding ID described above.

Creating a CloudWatch Events Rule and Target for GuardDuty

The following procedure shows how to use AWS CLI commands to create a CloudWatch Events rule and target for GuardDuty. Specifically, the procedure shows you how to create a rule that enables CloudWatch to send events for all findings that GuardDuty generates, and add an AWS Lambda function as a target for the rule.

Note
In addition to Lambda functions, GuardDuty and CloudWatch support the following target types: Amazon EC2 instances, Amazon Kinesis streams, Amazon ECS tasks, AWS Step Functions state machines, the run command, and built-in targets.

You can also create a CloudWatch Events rule and target for GuardDuty through the CloudWatch Events console. For more information and detailed steps, see Creating a CloudWatch Events Rule That Triggers on an Event. In the **Event Source** section, select **GuardDuty** for **Service name** and **GuardDuty Finding** for **Event Type**.

To create a rule and target

1. To create a rule that enables CloudWatch to send events for all findings that GuardDuty generates, run the following CloudWatch CLI command:

```
aws events put-rule --name Test --event-pattern "{\"source\":[\"aws.guardduty\"]}"
```
Important

You can further customize your rule so that it instructs CloudWatch to send events only for a subset of the GuardDuty-generated findings. This subset is based on the finding attribute(s) that are specified in the rule. For example, use the following CLI command to create a rule that enables CloudWatch to only send events for the GuardDuty findings with the severity of either 5.0 or 8.0:

```
aws events put-rule --name Test --event-pattern "{\"source\":[\"aws.guardduty\"],\"
detail-type\":[\"GuardDuty Finding\"],\"detail\":{\"severity\":[5.0,8.0]}}"
```

For this purpose, you can use any of the GuardDuty attributes that are supported for sorting findings. For more information, see GetFindings.

2. To attach a Lambda function as a target for the rule that you created in step 1, run the following CloudWatch CLI command:

```
aws events put-targets --rule Test --targets Id=1,Arn=arn:aws:lambda:us-east
-1:111122223333:function:<your_function>
```
Note

Make sure to replace <your_function> in the command above with your actual Lambda function for the GuardDuty events.

3. To add the permissions required to invoke the target, run the following Lambda CLI command:

```
aws lambda add-permission --function-name <your_function> --statement-id 1 --action '
lambda:InvokeFunction' --principal events.amazonaws.com
```
Note

Make sure to replace <your_function> in the command above with your actual Lambda function for the GuardDuty events.

Amazon GuardDuty API Reference

Amazon GuardDuty monitors the security of your AWS environment by analyzing and processing VPC Flow Logs and AWS CloudTrail event logs. This guide describes GuardDuty API operations.

Note

All GuardDuty actions are logged by Amazon CloudTrail. For more information, see Logging Amazon GuardDuty API Calls with AWS CloudTrail.

Topics

- AcceptInvitation
- ArchiveFindings
- CreateDetector
- CreateFilter
- CreateIPSet
- CreateMembers
- CreateSampleFindings
- CreateThreatIntelSet
- DeclineInvitations
- DeleteDetector
- DeleteFilter
- DeleteInvitations
- DeleteIPSet
- DeleteMembers
- DeleteThreatIntelSet
- DisassociateFromMasterAccount
- DisassociateMembers
- GetDetector
- GetFilter
- GetFindings
- GetFindingsStatistics
- GetInvitationsCount
- GetIPSet
- GetMasterAccount
- GetMembers
- GetThreatIntelSet
- InviteMembers
- ListDetectors
- ListFilters
- ListFindings
- ListInvitations
- ListIPSets
- ListMembers
- ListThreatIntelSets
- StartMonitoringMembers
- StopMonitoringMembers
- UnarchiveFindings
- UpdateDetector
- UpdateFilter
- UpdateFindingsFeedback
- UpdateIPSet
- UpdateThreatIntelSet

AcceptInvitation

Accepts the invitation to be monitored by a master GuardDuty account.

Request Syntax

```
1 POST https://<endpoint>/detector/{detectorId}/master
```

Body:

```
1 {
2     "detectorId": "string",
3     "masterId": "string",
4     "invitationId": "string"
5 }
```

Path Parameters

detectorID
The detector ID of the AWS account that is accepting an invitation to become a GuardDuty member account.
Type: String
Required: Yes

Request Parameters

The request accepts the following data in JSON format.

masterId
The account ID of the master GuardDuty account whose invitation you're accepting.
Type: String
Required: Yes

invitationId
The ID of the invitation that is sent to the AWS account by the GuardDuty master account.
Type: String
Required: Yes

Response Elements

If the action is successful, the service sends back an HTTP 200 response.

Errors

If the action is not successful, the service sends back an HTTP error response code along with detailed error information.

InvalidInputException

The request is rejected. An invalid or out-of-range value is specified as an input parameter.

HTTP Status Code: 400

InvalidInputException

The request is rejected. A required query or path parameters are not specified.

HTTP Status Code: 400

InvalidInputException

The request is rejected. One or more input parameters have invalid values.

HTTP Status Code: 400

InvalidInputException

The request is rejected. The parameter `detectorId` has an invalid value.

HTTP Status Code: 400

InvalidInputException

The request is rejected. The current account cannot accept an invitation from the specified account ID because the latter is a member of another master account.

HTTP Status Code: 400

InvalidInputException

The request is rejected. The current account cannot accept invitations because the account contains created, invited, or associated members.

HTTP Status Code: 400

InvalidInputException

The request is rejected. The current account cannot accept invitations because it is already a member of a master account.

HTTP Status Code: 400

InvalidInputException

The request is rejected. The current account has no pending invitation from the specified master account ID or is already a member of another master account.

HTTP Status Code: 400

InvalidInputException

The request is rejected. The specified handshake role of the specified member account ID cannot be assumed by GuardDuty on behalf of the specified master account ID.

HTTP Status Code: 400

LimitExceededException

The request is rejected. The input `detectorId` is not owned by the current account.

HTTP Status Code: 400

InternalException

Internal server error.

HTTP Status Code: 500

Example

Sample Request

```
1 POST /detector/a12abc34d567e8fa901bc2d34e56789f0/master HTTP/1.1
2 Host: guardduty.us-west-2.amazonaws.com
3 Accept-Encoding: identity
4 Content-Length: 80
5 Authorization: AUTHPARAMS
6 X-Amz-Date: 20180125T203032Z
7 User-Agent: aws-cli/1.14.29 Python/2.7.9 Windows/8 botocore/1.8.33
8 {
9     "masterId":"012345678901",
10    "invitationId":"84b097800250d17d1872b34c4daadcf5"
11 }
```

Sample Response

```
1 HTTP/1.1 200 OK
2 Content-Type: application/json
3 Content-Length: 0
4 Date: Thu, 25 Jan 2018 20:30:33 GMT
5 x-amzn-RequestId: 97dfbc58-020e-11e8-92b2-215719f46e03
6 X-Amzn-Trace-Id: sampled=0;root=1-5a6a3e69-ddfaf64f3fc7013f95e3c3f8
7 X-Cache: Miss from cloudfront
8 Via: 1.1 d98420743a69852491bbdea73f7680bd.cloudfront.net (CloudFront)
9 X-Amz-Cf-Id: mNPHSIIZh4O75j28b4jSZ6JaybkjuX3ek9Qu0EREyNYT19f-ZC9opg==
10 Connection: Keep-alive
```

ArchiveFindings

Archives Amazon GuardDuty findings that are specified by a list of finding IDs.

Important
Users from GuardDuty member accounts cannot run this API. Currently in GuardDuty, users from member accounts CANNOT archive findings either in their own accounts, or in their master's account, or in other member accounts.

Request Syntax

```
1 POST https://<endpoint>/detector/{detectorId}/findings/archive
```

Body:

```
1 {
2     "findingIds": [
3         "string"
4     ]
5 }
```

Path Parameters

detectorId
The detector ID that specifies the GuardDuty service whose findings you want to archive.
Required: Yes
Type: String

Request Parameters

The request accepts the following data in JSON format.

findingIds
The IDs of the findings that you want to archive.
Type: Array of strings. Minimum number of 0 items. Maximum number of 50 items.
Required: Yes

Response Elements

If the action is successful, the service sends back an HTTP 200 response.

Errors

If the action is not successful, the service sends back an HTTP error response code along with detailed error information.

InvalidInputException

The request is rejected. An invalid or out-of-range value is specified as an input parameter.

HTTP Status Code: 400

InvalidInputException

The request is rejected. The required query or path parameters are not specified.

HTTP Status Code: 400

InvalidInputException

The request is rejected. One or more input parameters have invalid values.

HTTP Status Code: 400

InvalidInputException

The request is rejected. The parameter `detectorId` has an invalid value.

HTTP Status Code: 400

InvalidInputException

The request is rejected. The number of requested finding IDs is out-of-bounds.

HTTP Status Code: 400

NoSuchEntityException

The request is rejected. The input `detectorId` is not owned by the current account.

HTTP Status Code: 400

AccessDeniedException

The request is rejected. The caller is not authorized to call this API.

HTTP Status Code: 400

InternalException

Internal server error.

HTTP Status Code: 500

Example

Sample Request

```
1 POST /detector/c6b0be64463ff852400d8ae5b2353866/findings/archive HTTP/1.1
2 Host: guardduty.us-west-2.amazonaws.com
3 Accept-Encoding: identity
4 Content-Length: 52
5 Authorization: AUTHPARAMS
6 X-Amz-Date: 20180209T231008Z
7 User-Agent: aws-cli/1.14.29 Python/2.7.9 Windows/8 botocore/1.8.33
8 {
9     "findingIds":[
10         "9cb0be64df8ba1df249c45eb8a0bf584"
11     ]
12 }
```

Sample Response

```
1 HTTP/1.1 200 OK
2 Content-Type: application/json
3 Content-Length: 0
4 Date: Fri, 09 Feb 2018 23:10:09 GMT
5 x-amzn-RequestId: 5fc7b08b-0dee-11e8-b559-79ec310d4e06
```

6 X-Amzn-Trace-Id: sampled=0;root=1-5a7e2a51-442c3de5468266edf3c048ca
7 X-Cache: Miss from cloudfront
8 Via: 1.1 51f2e50a0d2a5ee1d9c830bf417b2713.cloudfront.net (CloudFront)
9 X-Amz-Cf-Id: uEzj5jCFHxEGfKoTmB6Wgt8a3uM2JaXrEH0qzaT_JQ-rMDr-HdT9PA==
10 Connection: Keep-alive

CreateDetector

Creates a single Amazon GuardDuty detector. A detector is an object that represents the GuardDuty service. You must create a detector to enable GuardDuty.

Important
Currently, GuardDuty supports only one detector resource per AWS account per region.

Request Syntax

```
1 POST https://<endpoint>/detector
```

Body:

```
1 {
2     "enable" : "boolean"
3 }
```

Request Parameters

The request accepts the following data in JSON format.

enable
Specifies whether the detector is to be enabled.
Type: Boolean
Required: Yes

Response Syntax

Body:

```
1 {
2     "detectorId": "string"
3 }
```

Response Elements

If the action is successful, the service sends back an HTTP 200 response.

The following data is returned in JSON format by the service.

detectorId
The unique ID of the created detector.
Type: String

Errors

If the action is not successful, the service sends back an HTTP error response code along with detailed error information.

InvalidInputException

The request is rejected. An invalid or out-of-range value is specified as an input parameter.

HTTP Status Code: 400

InvalidInputException

The request is rejected. The required query or path parameters are not specified.

HTTP Status Code: 400

InvalidInputException

The request is rejected. One or more input parameters have invalid values.

HTTP Status Code: 400

AccessDeniedException

The request is rejected. You do not have the required `iam:CreateServiceLinkedRole` permission.

HTTP Status Code: 400

LimitExceededException

The request is rejected. A detector already exists for the current account.

HTTP Status Code: 400

InternalException

Internal server error.

HTTP Status Code: 500

Example

Sample Request

```
1 POST /detector HTTP/1.1
2 Host: guardduty.us-west-2.amazonaws.com
3 Accept-Encoding: identity
4 Content-Length: 0
5 Authorization: AUTHPARAMS
6 X-Amz-Date: 20180123T215330Z
7 User-Agent: aws-cli/1.14.29 Python/2.7.9 Windows/8 botocore/1.8.33
```

Sample Response

```
1 HTTP/1.1 200 OK
2 Content-Type: application/json
3 Content-Length: 49
4 Date: Tue, 23 Jan 2018 21:53:32 GMT
5 x-amzn-RequestId: da9e1c5b-0087-11e8-8012-7985c94ad5ec
6 X-Amzn-Trace-Id: sampled=0;root=1-5a67aedc-76d97a5c367f2eac94d40825
7 X-Cache: Miss from cloudfront
8 Via: 1.1 08df71188a92655a7dcd1bb872797741.cloudfront.net (CloudFront)
9 X-Amz-Cf-Id: kYGX5j6wkW7fneZ8ee602vqpr3JCuQqBHyyMdpTwG9JV3u0ybcdaNQ==
10 Connection: Keep-alive
11 {
12     "detectorId":"12abc34d567e8fa901bc2d34e56789f0"
13 }
```

CreateFilter

Creates a GuardDuty findings filter using the specified finding criteria.

Request Syntax

```
1 POST https://<endpoint>/detector/{detectorId}/filter
```

Body:

```
1  {
2      "name": "string",
3      "description": "string",
4      "findingCriteria": {
5      "criterion": [
6         "<field>": {
7             "gt": "integer",
8             "gte": "integer",
9             "lt": "integer",
10            "lte": "integer",
11            "eq": [
12                "string"
13            ],
14            "neq": [
15                "string"
16            ]
17         ]
18      }
19      "action": "[NOOP|ARCHIVE]",
20      "rank": "integer"
21  }
```

Path Parameters

detectorId
The ID of the detector that specifies the GuardDuty service whose findings you want to filter.
Type: String
Required: Yes

Request Parameters

The request accepts the following data in JSON format.

name
The name of the filter.
Type: String
Required: Yes

description
The description of the filter.
Type: String
Required: No

findingCriteria

Represents the criteria to be used in the filter for querying findings.

Type: FindingCriteria

Required: Yes

You can only use the following attributes to query findings:

[See the AWS documentation website for more details]

Gt

Represents the "greater than" condition to be applied to a single field when querying for findings.

Required: No

Gte

Represents the "greater than equal" condition to be applied to a single field when querying for findings.

Required: No

Lt

Represents the "less than" condition to be applied to a single field when querying for findings.

Required: No

Lte

Represents the "less than equal" condition to be applied to a single field when querying for findings.

Required: No

Eq

Represents the "equal to" condition to be applied to a single field when querying for findings.

Required: No

Neq

Represents the "not equal to" condition to be applied to a single field when querying for findings.

Required: No

action

Specifies the action that is to be applied to the findings that match the filter.

Type: Enum

Required: No

Valid values: NOOP | ARCHIVE

Default: NOOP

rank

Specifies the position of the filter in the list of current filters. Also specifies the order in which this filter is applied to the findings.

Type: Integer

Required: No

Constraints: Minimum value is 1 and maximum value is equal to the increment of the total number of current filters.

Default: 1

Response Syntax

```
1 {
2     "name": "string",
3 }
```

Response Elements

If the action is successful, the service sends back an HTTP 200 response.

The following data is returned in JSON format by the service.

name

The name of the successfully created filter.

Type: String

Errors

If the action is not successful, the service sends back an HTTP error response code along with detailed error information.

InvalidInputException

The request is rejected. The required query or path parameters are not specified.

HTTP Status Code: 400

InvalidInputException

The request is rejected. One or more input parameters have invalid values.

HTTP Status Code: 400

InvalidInputException

The request is rejected. The parameter `detectorId` has an invalid value.

HTTP Status Code: 400

InvalidInputException

The request is rejected. The parameter `name` has an invalid value.

HTTP Status Code: 400

InvalidInputException

The request is rejected. The parameter `description` has an invalid value.

HTTP Status Code: 400

InvalidInputException

The request is rejected. The parameter `findingCriteria` has an invalid value.

HTTP Status Code: 400

InvalidInputException

The request is rejected. The parameter `action` has an invalid value.

HTTP Status Code: 400

InvalidInputException

The request is rejected. The parameter `rank` has an invalid value.

HTTP Status Code: 400

NoSuchEntityException

The request is rejected. The input `detectorId` is not owned by the current account.

HTTP Status Code: 400

AccessDeniedException

The request is rejected. The caller is not authorized to call this API.

HTTP Status Code: 400

LimitExceededException

The request is rejected because filter limit has exceeded.

HTTP Status Code: 400

EntityAlreadyExistsException

The request is rejected because a filter with the given name already exists.

HTTP Status Code: 400

InternalException

Internal server error.

HTTP Status Code: 500

CreateIPSet

Creates an IPSet, which is a list of trusted IP addresses that have been whitelisted for highly secure communication with your AWS environment.

Important
Users from GuardDuty member accounts cannot run this API. Currently in GuardDuty, users from member accounts CANNOT upload and further manage IPSets. IPSets that are uploaded by the master account are imposed on GuardDuty functionality in its member accounts. For more information, see Managing AWS Accounts in Amazon GuardDuty.

Request Syntax

```
POST https://<endpoint>/detector/{detectorId}/ipset
```

Body:

```
{
    "name": "string",
    "location": "string",
    "format": "[TXT|STIX|OTX_CSV|ALIEN_VAULT|PROOF_POINT|FIRE_EYE]",
    "activate": "boolean"
}
```

Path Parameters

detectorId
The detector ID that specifies the GuardDuty service for which an IPSet is to be created.
Type: String
Required: Yes

Request Parameters

The request accepts the following data in JSON format.

name
The friendly name to identify the IPSet. This name is displayed in all findings that are triggered by activity that involves IP addresses included in this IPSet.
Type: String
Required: Yes

format
The format of the file that contains the IPSet.
Type: String. Valid values: TXT | STIX | OTX_CSV | ALIEN_VAULT | PROOF_POINT | FIRE_EYE
In your trusted IP lists and threat lists, IP addresses and CIDR ranges must appear one per line.
The following is a sample list in Plaintext format:

```
54.20.175.217
205.0.0.0/8
```

For more information, see Working with Trusted IP Lists and Threat Lists Required: Yes

location
The URI of the file that contains the IPSet.

Type: String
Required: Yes

activate
Specifies whether GuardDuty is to start using the uploaded IPSet.
Type: Boolean
Required: Yes

Response Syntax

```
1 {
2     "ipSetId": "string"
3 }
```

Response Elements

If the action is successful, the service sends back an HTTP 200 response.

The following data is returned in JSON format by the service.

ipSetId
The unique ID that specifies the newly created IPSet.
Type: String

Errors

If the action is not successful, the service returns an HTTP error response code along with detailed error information.

HTTP Status Code: 400

InvalidInputException

The request is rejected. The required query or path parameters are not specified.

HTTP Status Code: 400

InvalidInputException

The request is rejected. One or more input parameters have invalid values.

HTTP Status Code: 400

InvalidInputException

The request is rejected. The parameter `detectorId` has an invalid value.

HTTP Status Code: 400

InvalidInputException

The request is rejected. The parameter `name` has an invalid value.

HTTP Status Code: 400

InvalidInputException

The request is rejected. The parameter `location` has an invalid value.

HTTP Status Code: 400

InvalidInputException

The request is rejected. The parameter `format` has an invalid value.

HTTP Status Code: 400

InvalidInputException

The request is rejected. An invalid or out-of-range value is specified as an input parameter.

HTTP Status Code: 400

InvalidInputException

The request is rejected. Member accounts cannot manage IPSets or ThreatIntelSets.

HTTP Status Code: 400

NoSuchEntityException

The request is rejected. The input `detectorId` is not owned by the current account.

AccessDeniedException

The request is rejected. The caller is not authorized to call this API.

HTTP Status Code: 400

NoSuchEntityException

The request is rejected. No role was found.

HTTP Status Code: 400

BadRequestException

The request is rejected. The service can't assume the service role.

HTTP Status Code: 400

AccessDeniedException

The request is rejected. You do not have the required `iam:PutRolePolicy` permission.

HTTP Status Code: 400

BadRequestException

The request is rejected. The specified service role is not a service-linked role.

HTTP Status Code: 400

InternalException

Internal server error.

HTTP Status Code: 500

Example

Sample Request

```
1 POST /detector/12abc34d567e8fa901bc2d34e56789f0/ipset HTTP/1.1
2 Host: guardduty.us-west-2.amazonaws.com
3 Accept-Encoding: identity
4 Content-Length: 125
5 Authorization: AUTHPARAMS
6 X-Amz-Date: 20180124T000824Z
7 User-Agent: aws-cli/1.14.29 Python/2.7.9 Windows/8 botocore/1.8.33
8 {
```

```
 9     "format":"TXT",
10     "activate":true,
11     "location":"https://s3.amazonaws.com/guarddutylists/sample.txt",
12     "name":"ExampleIPSet"
13  }
```

Sample Response

```
 1  HTTP/1.1 200 OK
 2  Content-Type: application/json
 3  Content-Length: 46
 4  Date: Wed, 24 Jan 2018 00:08:34 GMT
 5  x-amzn-RequestId: b2890dcb-009a-11e8-b847-0dd5f510dc2a
 6  X-Amzn-Trace-Id: sampled=0;root=1-5a67ce79-a478009a74d2b2b17cba97f3
 7  X-Cache: Miss from cloudfront
 8  Via: 1.1 97c5dcf9c391508cdebbbfdcf304912f.cloudfront.net (CloudFront)
 9  X-Amz-Cf-Id: F6a_zK56EOZU_GODJVrzv94U9bH9ckLWXa0bCeHSbdaivK-WkTb77Q==
10  Connection: Keep-alive
11  {
12      "ipSetId":"0cb0141ab9fbde177613ab9436212e90"
13  }
```

CreateMembers

Creates member Amazon GuardDuty accounts in the current AWS account (which becomes the master GuardDuty account) that has GuardDuty enabled.

Request Syntax

```
1 POST https://<endpoint>/detector/{detectorId}/member
```

Body:

```
1 {
2     "accountDetails": [
3         {
4             "accountId": "string",
5             "email": "string"
6         }
7     ]
8 }
```

Path Parameters

detectorID
The detector ID of the GuardDuty account where you want to create member accounts.
Type: String
Required: Yes

Request Parameters

The request accepts the following data in JSON format.

accountDetails
A list of account ID and email address pairs of the accounts that you want to associate with the master GuardDuty account.
Type: Array of strings. Minimum number of items: 1. Maximum number of items: 50.
Required: Yes
accountID
The AWS account ID.
Type: String
Required: Yes
email
The email address of the AWS account.
Type: String
Required: Yes

Response Syntax

```
1 {
2     "unprocessedAccounts": [
3         {
4             "accountId": "string",
5             "result": "string"
```

```
6        }
7    ]
8 }
```

Response Elements

If the action is successful, the service sends back an HTTP 200 response.

The following data is returned in JSON format by the service.

unprocessedAccounts
A list of account ID and email address pairs of the AWS accounts that could not be processed.
Type: Array of strings
accountID
The ID of the AWS account that could not be processed.
Type: String
result
The reason why the AWS account could not be processed.
Type: String

Errors

If the action is not successful, the service sends back an HTTP error response code along with detailed error information.

InvalidInputException

The request is rejected. The current account cannot create members because it is already a member of another master account.

HTTP Status Code: 200

InvalidInputException

The request is rejected. An account cannot become a member of itself.

HTTP Status Code: 200

InvalidInputException

The request is rejected. The specified account ID is already a member or associated member of the current account.

HTTP Status Code: 200

LimitExceededException

The request is rejected. The current account cannot create more members because it cannot exceed the maximum number of allowed members.

HTTP Status Code: 200

InvalidInputException

The request is rejected. An invalid or out-of-range value is specified as an input parameter.

HTTP Status Code: 400

InvalidInputException

The request is rejected. The required query or path parameters are not specified.

HTTP Status Code: 400

InvalidInputException

The request is rejected. One or more input parameters have invalid values.

HTTP Status Code: 400

InvalidInputException

The request is rejected. The parameter `detectorId` has an invalid value.

HTTP Status Code: 400

NoSuchEntityException

The request is rejected. The input `detectorId` is not owned by the current account.

HTTP Status Code: 400

InternalException

Internal server error.

HTTP Status Code: 500

Example

Sample Request

```
1 POST /detector/12abc34d567e8fa901bc2d34e56789f0/member HTTP/1.1
2 Host: guardduty.us-west-2.amazonaws.com
3 Accept-Encoding: identity
4 Content-Length: 84
5 Authorization: AUTHPARAMS
6 X-Amz-Date: 20180125T193018Z
7 User-Agent: aws-cli/1.14.29 Python/2.7.9 Windows/8 botocore/1.8.33
8 {
9    "accountDetails":[
10      {
11        "email":"guarddutymember@amazon.com",
12        "accountId":"123456789012"
13      }
14    ]
15 }
```

Sample Response

```
1 HTTP/1.1 200 OK
2 Content-Type: application/json
3 Content-Length: 26
4 Date: Thu, 25 Jan 2018 19:30:19 GMT
5 x-amzn-RequestId: 2ddb8329-0206-11e8-a10a-75feffd08476
6 X-Amzn-Trace-Id: sampled=0;root=1-5a6a304b-0bc475fb7f9beaf25dc8a6a4
7 X-Cache: Miss from cloudfront
8 Via: 1.1 3a9dca02f1ba6ecd49fee9a3ca7fcb81.cloudfront.net (CloudFront)
9 X-Amz-Cf-Id: nujl7jYlNFfsX25GF6wgrCTyrwmys-SclGlZh2QIZFzxznX53yYYTw==
10 Connection: Keep-alive
11 {
12    "unprocessedAccounts":[
13
14    ]
15 }
```

CreateSampleFindings

Creates sample findings of the types that are specified by a list of Amazon GuardDuty finding types. If NULL is specified for `findingTypes`, the operation creates sample findings of all supported GuardDuty finding types.

Request Syntax

```
1 POST https://<endpoint>/detector/{detectorId}/findings/create
```

Body:

```
1 {
2     "findingTypes": [
3         {
4             "findingType": "string",
5         }
6     ]
7 }
```

Path Parameters

detectorId
The ID of the GuardDuty service where you want to create sample findings.
Required: Yes
Type: String

Request Parameters

The request accepts the following data in JSON format.

findingTypes
The list of GuardDuty finding types that specifies what types of sample findings that you want to create.
Required: Yes
Type: Array of strings
Constraints: Minimum length of 0. Maximum length of 50.
findingType
The type of the GuardDuty finding.
Type: String

Response Elements

If the action is successful, the service sends back an HTTP 200 response.

Errors

If the action is not successful, the service sends back an HTTP error response code along with detailed error information.

InvalidInputException

The request is rejected. An invalid or out-of-range value is specified as an input parameter.

HTTP Status Code: 400

InvalidInputException

The request is rejected. The required query or path parameters are not specified.

HTTP Status Code: 400

InvalidInputException

The request is rejected. One or more input parameters have invalid values.

HTTP Status Code: 400

InvalidInputException

The request is rejected. The parameter `detectorId` has an invalid value.

HTTP Status Code: 400

InvalidInputException

The request is rejected. An invalid finding type is specified.

HTTP Status Code: 400

NoSuchEntityException

The request is rejected. The input `detectorId` is not owned by the current account.

HTTP Status Code: 400

InternalException

Internal server error.

HTTP Status Code: 500

Example

Sample Request

```
1 POST /detector/c6b0be64463ff852400d8ae5b2353866/findings/create HTTP/1.1
2 Host: guardduty.us-west-2.amazonaws.com
3 Accept-Encoding: identity
4 Content-Length: 0
5 Authorization: AUTHPARAMS
6 X-Amz-Date: 20180209T225730Z
7 User-Agent: aws-cli/1.14.29 Python/2.7.9 Windows/8 botocore/1.8.33
```

Sample Response

```
1 HTTP/1.1 200 OK
2 Content-Type: application/json
3 Content-Length: 0
4 Date: Fri, 09 Feb 2018 22:57:32 GMT
5 x-amzn-RequestId: 9c2bd04f-0dec-11e8-9ce5-1d60637acb70
6 X-Amzn-Trace-Id: sampled=0;root=1-5a7e275b-e03cf47efbf2e2aea8199ebf
7 X-Cache: Miss from cloudfront
8 Via: 1.1 27a783405519f49942e72a6ed75f783f.cloudfront.net (CloudFront)
9 X-Amz-Cf-Id: eat7We8tGOkIFZ9TQ6UEcGQQZI17OTIMUcRSR6GrcjbLmHEJWszspQ==
10 Connection: Keep-alive
```

CreateThreatIntelSet

Creates a ThreatIntelSet. A ThreatIntelSet consists of known malicious IP addresses. GuardDuty generates findings based on the ThreatIntelSet.

Important
Users from GuardDuty member accounts cannot run this API. Currently in GuardDuty, users from member accounts CANNOT upload and further manage ThreatIntelSets. ThreatIntelSets that are uploaded by the master account are imposed on GuardDuty functionality in its member accounts. For more information, see Managing AWS Accounts in Amazon GuardDuty.

Request Syntax

```
1 POST https://<endpoint>/detector/{detectorId}/threatintelset
```

Body:

```
1 {
2     "name": "string",
3     "location": "string",
4     "format": "[TXT|STIX|OTX_CSV|ALIEN_VAULT|PROOF_POINT|FIRE_EYE]",
5     "activate": "boolean"
6 }
```

Path Parameters

detectorId
The detector ID that specifies the GuardDuty service for which you want to create a ThreatIntelSet.
Type: String
Required: Yes

Request Parameters

The request accepts the following data in JSON format.

name
A friendly ThreatIntelSet name. The name is displayed in all findings that are generated by activity that involves IP addresses included in this ThreatIntelSet.
Type: String
Required: Yes

format
The format of the file that contains the ThreatIntelSet.
Type: String. Valid values: `TXT` | `STIX` | `OTX_CSV` | `ALIEN_VAULT` | `PROOF_POINT` | `FIRE_EYE`
In your trusted IP lists and threat lists, IP addresses and CIDR ranges must appear one per line.
The following is a sample list in Plaintext format:

```
1 54.20.175.217
2 205.0.0.0/8
```

For more information, see Working with Trusted IP Lists and Threat Lists Required: Yes

location
The URI of the file that contains the ThreatIntelSet.

Type: String
Required: Yes

activate
Specifies whether GuardDuty is to start using the created ThreatIntelSet.
Type: Boolean
Required: Yes

Response Syntax

```
1 {
2     "threatIntelSetId": "string"
3 }
```

Response Elements

If the action is successful, the service sends back an HTTP 200 response.

The following data is returned in JSON format by the service.

threatIntelSetId
The unique ID that specifies the newly created ThreatIntelSet.
Type: String

Errors

If the action is not successful, the service sends back an HTTP error response code along with detailed error information.

InvalidInputException

The request is rejected. An invalid or out-of-range value is specified as an input parameter.

HTTP Status Code: 400

InvalidInputException

The request is rejected. The required query or path parameters are not specified.

HTTP Status Code: 400

InvalidInputException

The request is rejected. One or more input parameters have invalid values.

HTTP Status Code: 400

InvalidInputException

The request is rejected. The parameter `name` has an invalid value.

HTTP Status Code: 400

InvalidInputException

The request is rejected. The parameter `location` has an invalid value.

HTTP Status Code: 400

InvalidInputException

The request is rejected. The parameter `format` has an invalid value.

HTTP Status Code: 400

InvalidInputException

The request is rejected. The parameter `detectorId` has an invalid value.

HTTP Status Code: 400

NoSuchEntityException

The request is rejected. The input `detectorId` is not owned by the current account.

HTTP Status Code: 400

AccessDeniedException

The request is rejected. The caller is not authorized to call this API.

HTTP Status Code: 400

NoSuchEntityException

The request is rejected. No role was found.

HTTP Status Code: 400

InvalidInputException

The request is rejected. Member accounts cannot manage IPSets or ThreatIntelSets.

HTTP Status Code: 400

BadRequestException

The request is rejected. The service can't assume the service role.

HTTP Status Code: 400

AccessDeniedException

The request is rejected. You do not have the required `iam:PutRolePolicy` permission.

HTTP Status Code: 400

BadRequestException

The request is rejected. The specified service role is not a service-linked role.

HTTP Status Code: 400

InternalException

Internal server error.

HTTP Status Code: 500

Example

Sample Request

```
1 POST /detector/12abc34d567e8fa901bc2d34e56789f0/threatintelset HTTP/1.1
2 Host: guardduty.us-west-2.amazonaws.com
3 Accept-Encoding: identity
4 Content-Length: 142
5 Authorization: AUTHPARAMS
6 X-Amz-Date: 20180124T194824Z
7 User-Agent: aws-cli/1.14.29 Python/2.7.9 Windows/8 botocore/1.8.33
8 {
```

```
 9     "format":"TXT",
10     "activate":true,
11     "location":"https://s3.amazonaws.com/guarddutylists/threatintelset.txt",
12     "name":"ThreatIntelSet"
13  }
```

Sample Response

```
 1  HTTP/1.1 200 OK
 2  Content-Type: application/json
 3  Content-Length: 55
 4  Date: Wed, 24 Jan 2018 19:48:36 GMT
 5  x-amzn-RequestId: 8af4b349-013f-11e8-8f6b-e37a19b6d996
 6  X-Amzn-Trace-Id: sampled=0;root=1-5a68e30a-ffc9e16710a559d971138391
 7  X-Cache: Miss from cloudfront
 8  Via: 1.1 7f3f42df8af148df1f9f1ee7175987ad.cloudfront.net (CloudFront)
 9  X-Amz-Cf-Id: KPy-b4jZhTp_ahwtcYga-g7K_Urr1QFGL3lIEnZSR6KpfAQ1vxTE3A==
10  Connection: Keep-alive
11  {
12      "threatIntelSetId":"8cb094db7082fd0db09479755d215dba"
13  }
```

DeclineInvitations

Declines invitations that are sent to this AWS account (invitee) by the AWS accounts (inviters) that are specified by the account IDs.

Request Syntax

```
1  POST https://<endpoint>/invitation/decline
```

Body:

```
1  {
2      "accountIds": [
3          {
4              "accountId": "string"
5          }
6      ]
7  }
```

Request Parameters

The request accepts the following data in JSON format.

accountIds
A list of account IDs specifying accounts whose invitations to GuardDuty you want to decline.
Type: Array of strings
Required: Yes
accountID
The AWS account ID.
Type: String

Response Syntax

```
1  {
2      "unprocessedAccounts": [
3          {
4              "accountId": "string",
5              "result": "string"
6          }
7      ]
8  }
```

Response Elements

If the action is successful, the service sends back an HTTP 200 response.

The following data is returned in JSON format by the service.

unprocessedAccounts
A list of account ID and email address pairs of the AWS accounts that could not be processed.
Type: Array of strings
accountID
The ID of the AWS account that could not be processed.
Type: String

result

The reason why the AWS account could not be processed.

Type: String

Errors

If the action is not successful, the service sends back an HTTP error response code along with detailed error information.

InvalidInputException

The request is rejected. An invalid or out-of-range value is specified as an input parameter.

HTTP Status Code: 400

InvalidInputException

The request is rejected. The required query or path parameters are not specified.

HTTP Status Code: 400

InvalidInputException

The request is rejected. One or more input parameters have invalid values.

HTTP Status Code: 400

InternalException

Internal server error.

HTTP Status Code: 500

Example

Sample Request

```
1 POST /invitation/decline HTTP/1.1
2 Host: guardduty.us-west-2.amazonaws.com
3 Accept-Encoding: identity
4 Content-Length: 32
5 Authorization: AUTHPARAMS
6 X-Amz-Date: 20180209T212220Z
7 User-Agent: aws-cli/1.14.29 Python/2.7.9 Windows/8 botocore/1.8.33
8 {
9     "accountIds":[
10        "123456789012"
11    ]
12 }
```

Sample Response

```
1 HTTP/1.1 200 OK
2 Content-Type: application/json
3 Content-Length: 26
4 Date: Fri, 09 Feb 2018 21:22:22 GMT
5 x-amzn-RequestId: 50d4524e-0ddf-11e8-8662-ef6b8065279d
6 X-Amzn-Trace-Id: sampled=0;root=1-5a7e110d-59812fd97e6d69b6d0444902
7 X-Cache: Miss from cloudfront
8 Via: 1.1 13fbcc8fa3dbc202089a58be1b399e76.cloudfront.net (CloudFront)
```

```
 9 X-Amz-Cf-Id: tc1MUaEI2G-yoIMgPEZlgCLmDvwMuJXiJF6LrMoFVjjqcGOEJPdvBQ==
10 Connection: Keep-alive
11 {
12    "unprocessedAccounts":[
13
14    ]
15 }
```

DeleteDetector

Deletes the Amazon GuardDuty detector that is specified by the detector ID.

Request Syntax

```
1 DELETE https://<endpoint>/detector/{detectorId}
```

Body:

```
1 detectorId : "string"
```

Path Parameters

detectorId
The unique ID that specifies the detector that you want to delete.
Type: String
Required: Yes

Response Elements

If the action is successful, the service sends back an HTTP 200 response.

Errors

If the action is not successful, the service sends back an HTTP error response code along with detailed error information.

InvalidInputException

The request is rejected. An invalid or out-of-range value is specified as an input parameter.

HTTP Status Code: 400

InvalidInputException

The request is rejected. The required query or path parameters are not specified.

HTTP Status Code: 400

InvalidInputException

The request is rejected. One or more input parameters have invalid values.

HTTP Status Code: 400

InvalidInputException

The request is rejected. The parameter `detectorId` has an invalid value.

HTTP Status Code: 400

InvalidInputException

The request is rejected. The current account cannot delete the detector while it has invited or associated members.

HTTP Status Code: 400

NoSuchEntityException

The request is rejected. The input `detectorId` is not owned by the current account.

HTTP Status Code: 400

InternalException

Internal server error.

HTTP Status Code: 500

Example

Sample Request

```
1 DELETE /detector/12abc34d567e8fa901bc2d34e56789f0 HTTP/1.1
2 Host: guardduty.us-west-2.amazonaws.com
3 Accept-Encoding: identity
4 Content-Length: 0
5 Authorization: AUTHPARAMS
6 X-Amz-Date: 20180123T232121Z
7 User-Agent: aws-cli/1.14.29 Python/2.7.9 Windows/8 botocore/1.8.33
```

Sample Response

```
1  HTTP/1.1 200 OK
2  Content-Type: application/json
3  Content-Length: 0
4  Date: Tue, 23 Jan 2018 23:21:22 GMT
5  x-amzn-RequestId: 1fe65a9d-0094-11e8-8344-4bf20881d099
6  X-Amzn-Trace-Id: sampled=0;root=1-5a67c372-77952f70fa2c7ec0c02de331
7  X-Cache: Miss from cloudfront
8  Via: 1.1 840717da68adc4ace0e2050590aef6c5.cloudfront.net (CloudFront)
9  X-Amz-Cf-Id: 4DHXuXpYnaCtVtK0oZlEy41MbwZkEF2KKjT-m0lMqA8vgghBNIEcGA==
10 Connection: Keep-alive
```

DeleteFilter

Deletes the filter specified by the filter name.

Request Syntax

```
1 DELETE https://<endpoint>/detector/{detectorId}/filter/<filter-name>
```

Body:

```
1 detectorId : "string"
```

Path Parameters

detectorId
The unique ID that specifies the detector where you want to delete a filter.
Type: String
Required: Yes

filterName
The name of the filter
Type: String
Required: Yes

Response Elements

If the action is successful, the service sends back an HTTP 200 response.

Errors

If the action is not successful, the service sends back an HTTP error response code along with detailed error information.

InvalidInputException

The request is rejected. An invalid or out-of-range value is specified as an input parameter.

HTTP Status Code: 400

InvalidInputException

The request is rejected. The required query or path parameters are not specified.

HTTP Status Code: 400

InvalidInputException

The request is rejected. One or more input parameters have invalid values.

HTTP Status Code: 400

InvalidInputException

The request is rejected. The parameter `detectorId` has an invalid value.

HTTP Status Code: 400

InvalidInputException

The request is rejected. The parameter **name** has an invalid value.

HTTP Status Code: 400

NoSuchEntityException

The request is rejected. The input `detectorId` is not owned by the current account.

HTTP Status Code: 400

NoSuchEntityException

The request is rejected. The input `name` is not owned by the current account.

HTTP Status Code: 400

InternalException

Internal server error.

HTTP Status Code: 500

DeleteInvitations

Deletes invitations that are sent to this AWS account (invitee) by the AWS accounts (inviters) that are specified by their account IDs.

Request Syntax

```
1 POST https://<endpoint>/invitation/delete
```

Body:

```
1 {
2     "accountIds": [
3         {
4             "accountId": "string"
5         }
6     ]
7 }
```

Request Parameters

The request accepts the following data in JSON format.

accountIds
A list of account IDs specifying accounts whose invitations to GuardDuty you want to delete.
Type: Array of strings
Required: Yes
accountID
The AWS account ID.
Type: String

Response Syntax

```
1 {
2     "unprocessedAccounts": [
3         {
4             "accountId": "string",
5             "result": "string"
6         }
7     ]
8 }
```

Response Elements

If the action is successful, the service sends back an HTTP 200 response.

The following data is returned in JSON format by the service.

unprocessedAccounts
A list of account ID and email address pairs of the AWS accounts that could not be processed.
Type: Array of strings
accountID
The ID of the AWS account that could not be processed.
Type: String

result

The reason why the AWS account could not be processed.

Type: String

Errors

If the action is not successful, the service sends back an HTTP error response code along with detailed error information.

InvalidInputException

The request is rejected. The current account cannot delete the invitation from the specified master account ID because it is still associated to it or has not declined the invitation yet.

HTTP Status Code: 200

InvalidInputException

The request is rejected. An invalid or out-of-range value is specified as an input parameter.

HTTP Status Code: 400

InvalidInputException

The request is rejected. The required query or path parameters are not specified.

HTTP Status Code: 400

InvalidInputException

The request is rejected. One or more input parameters have invalid values.

HTTP Status Code: 400

InternalException

Internal server error.

HTTP Status Code: 500

Example

Sample Request

```
1 POST /invitation/delete HTTP/1.1
2 Host: guardduty.us-west-2.amazonaws.com
3 Accept-Encoding: identity
4 Content-Length: 32
5 Authorization: AUTHPARAMS
6 X-Amz-Date: 20180209T212908Z
7 User-Agent: aws-cli/1.14.29 Python/2.7.9 Windows/8 botocore/1.8.33
8 {
9     "accountIds":[
10        "123456789012"
11     ]
12 }
```

Sample Response

```
1  HTTP/1.1 200 OK
2  Content-Type: application/json
3  Content-Length: 26
4  Date: Fri, 09 Feb 2018 21:29:09 GMT
5  x-amzn-RequestId: 43a71a1a-0de0-11e8-8dbe-7f113b66b9c1
6  X-Amzn-Trace-Id: sampled=0;root=1-5a7e12a5-8e3f17ba0cdd7d2a87fe74e8
7  X-Cache: Miss from cloudfront
8  Via: 1.1 a2a7227d0a99f50bffb8ba79de64ab0f.cloudfront.net (CloudFront)
9  X-Amz-Cf-Id: acpQcNsnYmk1zKcvkck5cGCYl-35rw5wZvzlWxRrvzNbYV8oj9RcIg==
10 Connection: Keep-alive
11 {
12     "unprocessedAccounts":[
13
14     ]
15 }
```

DeleteIPSet

Deletes the IPSet that is specified by the IPSet ID.

Important
Users from GuardDuty member accounts cannot run this API. Currently in GuardDuty, users from member accounts CANNOT upload and further manage IPSets. IPSets that are uploaded by the master account are imposed on GuardDuty functionality in its member accounts. For more information, see Managing AWS Accounts in Amazon GuardDuty.

Request Syntax

```
1 DELETE https://<endpoint>/detector/{detectorId}/ipset/{ipSetId}
```

Body:

```
1 detectoId : "string"
2 ipSetId : "string"
```

Path Parameters

The request accepts the following data in JSON format.

detectorId
The detector ID that specifies the GuardDuty service whose IPSet you want to delete.
Type: String
Required: Yes

ipSetId
The unique ID that specifies the IPSet that you want to delete.
Type: String
Required: Yes

Response Syntax

If the action is successful, the service sends back an HTTP 200 response.

Errors

If the action is not successful, the service sends back an HTTP error response code along with detailed error information.

InvalidInputException

The request is rejected. An invalid or out-of-range value is specified as an input parameter.

HTTP Status Code: 400

InvalidInputException

The request is rejected. The required query or path parameters are not specified.

HTTP Status Code: 400

InvalidInputException

The request is rejected. One or more input parameters have invalid values.

HTTP Status Code: 400

InvalidInputException

The request is rejected. The parameter `detectorId` has an invalid value.

HTTP Status Code: 400

InvalidInputException

The request is rejected. An invalid `ipSetId` is specified.

HTTP Status Code: 400

NoSuchEntityException

The request is rejected. The input `detectorId` is not owned by the current account.

InvalidInputException

The request is rejected. Member accounts cannot manage IPSets or ThreatIntelSets.

HTTP Status Code: 400

HTTP Status Code: 400

NoSuchEntityException

The request is rejected. An invalid `ipSetId` is specified.

HTTP Status Code: 400

AccessDeniedException

The request is rejected. The caller is not authorized to call this API.

HTTP Status Code: 400

InternalException

Internal server error.

HTTP Status Code: 500

Example

Sample Request

```
1 DELETE /detector/12abc34d567e8fa901bc2d34e56789f0/ipset/0cb0141ab9fbde177613ab9436212e90 HTTP
    /1.1
2 Host: guardduty.us-west-2.amazonaws.com
3 Accept-Encoding: identity
4 Content-Length: 0
5 Authorization: AUTHPARAMS
6 X-Amz-Date: 20180124T003336Z
7 User-Agent: aws-cli/1.14.29 Python/2.7.9 Windows/8 botocore/1.8.33
```

Sample Response

```
1 HTTP/1.1 200 OK
2 Content-Type: application/json
3 Content-Length: 0
4 Date: Wed, 24 Jan 2018 00:33:38 GMT
5 x-amzn-RequestId: 37ff4946-009e-11e8-8cd0-dfa2161e90c7
6 X-Amzn-Trace-Id: sampled=0;root=1-5a67d461-8a28ae442fc2780e9f9db40f
```

7 X-Cache: Miss from cloudfront
8 Via: 1.1 2a7e9ec6f25ccbf79b1adfa129de8f9c.cloudfront.net (CloudFront)
9 X-Amz-Cf-Id: eMcCNyWbQT9FNOhqD-LG11jGEpaY8YH1kpQW3OYfDM9BQfnlu6uuoA==
10 Connection: Keep-alive

DeleteMembers

Deletes the Amazon GuardDuty member accounts that are specified by the account IDs.

Request Syntax

```
1 POST https://<endpoint>/detector/{detectorId}/member/delete
```

Body:

```
1 {
2     "accountIds": [
3         {
4             "accountId": "string"
5         }
6     ]
7 }
```

Path Parameters

detectorID
The detector ID of the GuardDuty service whose member accounts you want to delete.
Type: String
Required: Yes

Request Parameters

The request accepts the following data in JSON format.

accountIds
A list of account IDs of the GuardDuty member accounts that you want to delete.
Type: Array of strings
Required: Yes
accountID
AWS account ID.
Type: String

Response Syntax

```
1 {
2     "unprocessedAccounts": [
3         {
4             "accountId": "string",
5             "result": "string"
6         }
7     ]
8 }
```

Response Elements

If the action is successful, the service sends back an HTTP 200 response.

The service returns the following data is returned in JSON format.

unprocessedAccounts
A list of account ID and email address pairs of the AWS accounts that could not be processed.
Type: Array of strings
accountID
The ID of the AWS account that could not be processed.
Type: String
result
The reason why the AWS account could not be processed.
Type: String

Errors

If the action is not successful, the service sends back an HTTP error response code along with detailed error information.

InvalidInputException

The request is rejected. The current account cannot delete the specified member account ID because it is still associated to it.

HTTP Status Code: 200

InvalidInputException

The request is rejected. An invalid or out-of-range value is specified as an input parameter.

HTTP Status Code: 400

InvalidInputException

The request is rejected. The required query or path parameters are not specified.

HTTP Status Code: 400

InvalidInputException

The request is rejected. One or more input parameters have invalid values.

HTTP Status Code: 400

InvalidInputException

The request is rejected. The parameter `detectorId` has an invalid value.

HTTP Status Code: 400

NoSuchEntryException

The request is rejected. The input `detectorId` is not owned by the current account.

HTTP Status Code: 400

InternalException

Internal server error.

HTTP Status Code: 500

Example

Sample Request

```
1 POST /detector/26b092acdf3e60c625b69013f7488f7b/member/delete HTTP/1.1
2 Host: guardduty.us-west-2.amazonaws.com
3 Accept-Encoding: identity
4 Content-Length: 32
5 Authorization: AUTHPARAMS
6 X-Amz-Date: 20180209T220100Z
7 User-Agent: aws-cli/1.14.29 Python/2.7.9 Windows/8 botocore/1.8.33
8 {
9   "accountIds":[
10       "123456789012"
11   ]
12 }
```

Sample Response

```
1 HTTP/1.1 200 OK
2 Content-Type: application/json
3 Content-Length: 26
4 Date: Fri, 09 Feb 2018 22:01:01 GMT
5 x-amzn-RequestId: b7409e55-0de4-11e8-aa1d-17f6b1e5e6f5
6 X-Amzn-Trace-Id: sampled=0;root=1-5a7e1a1d-8736f50418456d404294b219
7 X-Cache: Miss from cloudfront
8 Via: 1.1 b2532cb29a55e8fe8106a4a9a9241592.cloudfront.net (CloudFront)
9 X-Amz-Cf-Id: yZC2KsBzimqUgjOxPaamXSKWpXmMlFOIOSbEhNamaGRNwkXzaf50yQ==
10 Connection: Keep-alive
11 {
12   "unprocessedAccounts":[
13
14   ]
15 }
```

DeleteThreatIntelSet

Deletes the ThreatIntelSet that is specified by the ThreatIntelSet ID.

Important
Users from GuardDuty member accounts cannot run this API. Currently in GuardDuty, users from member accounts CANNOT upload and further manage ThreatIntelSets. ThreatIntelSets that are uploaded by the master account are imposed on GuardDuty functionality in its member accounts. For more information, see Managing AWS Accounts in Amazon GuardDuty.

Request Syntax

```
1 DELETE https://<endpoint>/detector/{detectorId}/threatintelset/{threatIntelSetId}
```

Body:

```
1 detectorId : "string"
2 threatIntelSetId : "string"
```

Path Parameters

The request accepts the following data in JSON format.

detectorId
The detector ID that specifies the GuardDuty service whose `ThreatIntelSet` you want to delete.
Type: String
Required: Yes

threatIntelSetId
The unique ID that specifies the `ThreatIntelSet` that you want to delete.
Type: String
Required: Yes

Response Syntax

If the action is successful, the service sends back an HTTP 200 response.

Errors

If the action is not successful, the service sends back an HTTP error response code along with detailed error information.

InvalidInputException

The request is rejected. An invalid or out-of-range value is specified as an input parameter.

HTTP Status Code: 400

InvalidInputException

The request is rejected. The required query or path parameters are not specified.

HTTP Status Code: 400

InvalidInputException

The request is rejected. One or more input parameters have invalid values.

HTTP Status Code: 400

InvalidInputException

The request is rejected. The parameter `detectorId` has an invalid value.

HTTP Status Code: 400

InvalidInputException

The request is rejected. An invalid `threatIntelSetId` is specified.

HTTP Status Code: 400

InvalidInputException

The request is rejected. Member accounts cannot manage IPSets or ThreatIntelSets.

HTTP Status Code: 400

NoSuchEntityException

The request is rejected. The input `detectorId` is not owned by the current account.

HTTP Status Code: 400

NoSuchEntityException

The request is rejected. An invalid `threatIntelSetId` is specified.

HTTP Status Code: 400

AccessDeniedException

The request is rejected. The caller is not authorized to call this API.

HTTP Status Code: 400

InternalException

Internal server error.

HTTP Status Code: 500

Example

Sample Request

```
1 DELETE /detector/12abc34d567e8fa901bc2d34e56789f0/threatintelset/8
    cb094db7082fd0db09479755d215dba HTTP/1.1
2 Host: guardduty.us-west-2.amazonaws.com
3 Accept-Encoding: identity
4 Content-Length: 0
5 Authorization: AUTHPARAMS
6 X-Amz-Date: 20180124T212824Z
7 User-Agent: aws-cli/1.14.29 Python/2.7.9 Windows/8 botocore/1.8.33
```

Sample Response

```
1 HTTP/1.1 200 OK
2 Content-Type: application/json
3 Content-Length: 0
4 Date: Wed, 24 Jan 2018 21:28:26 GMT
5 x-amzn-RequestId: 8330e867-014d-11e8-b00e-f1d94214241f
6 X-Amzn-Trace-Id: sampled=0;root=1-5a68fa7a-6254473316398a8e7e769f64
```

```
7 X-Cache: Miss from cloudfront
8 Via: 1.1 85ddca57b96353e9e4cd2660cf65d9da.cloudfront.net (CloudFront)
9 X-Amz-Cf-Id: RntOBwBWFz8ljwXOrdnWfXXfJz12nRQHOiHngFq8fKrgW_b7K5iL4Q==
10 Connection: Keep-alive
```

DisassociateFromMasterAccount

Disassociates the current Amazon GuardDuty member account from its master account.

Request Syntax

```
1 POST https://<endpoint>/detector/{detectorId}/master/disassociate
```

Body:

```
1 detectorId : "string"
```

Path Parameters

The request accepts the following data in JSON format.

detectorID
The detector ID of the GuardDuty member account that wants to disassociate from its GuardDuty master account.
Type: String
Required: Yes

Response Elements

If the action is successful, the service sends back an HTTP 200 response.

Errors

If the action is not successful, the service sends back an HTTP error response code along with detailed error information.

InvalidInputException

The request is rejected. An invalid or out-of-range value is specified as an input parameter.

HTTP Status Code: 400

InvalidInputException

The request is rejected. The required query or path parameters are not specified.

HTTP Status Code: 400

InvalidInputException

The request is rejected. One or more input parameters have invalid values.

HTTP Status Code: 400

InvalidInputException

The request is rejected. The parameter `detectorId` has an invalid value.

HTTP Status Code: 400

InvalidInputException

The request is rejected. The current account is not associated with a master account.

HTTP Status Code: 400

NoSuchEntityException

The request is rejected. The input `detectorId` is not owned by the current account.

HTTP Status Code: 400

InternalException

Internal server error.

HTTP Status Code: 500

Example

Sample Request

```
1 POST /detector/12abc34d567e8fa901bc2d34e56789f0/master/disassociate HTTP/1.1
2 Host: guardduty.us-west-2.amazonaws.com
3 Accept-Encoding: identity
4 Content-Length: 0
5 Authorization: AUTHPARAMS
6 X-Amz-Date: 20180125T204326Z
7 User-Agent: aws-cli/1.14.29 Python/2.7.9 Windows/8 botocore/1.8.33
```

Sample Response

```
1  HTTP/1.1 200 OK
2  Content-Type: application/json
3  Content-Length: 0
4  Date: Thu, 25 Jan 2018 20:43:27 GMT
5  x-amzn-RequestId: 651fdfcb-0210-11e8-acaf-711608dc8498
6  X-Amzn-Trace-Id: sampled=0;root=1-5a6a416f-a0b7bcb94c74288c20bced1c
7  X-Cache: Miss from cloudfront
8  Via: 1.1 16d2657cebef5191828b055567b4efeb.cloudfront.net (CloudFront)
9  X-Amz-Cf-Id: iMpzmm9iLQIj7_dDe9wu6KZNFFhmGyDMpPYcUZevrJBsNHhbnjxGtA==
10 Connection: Keep-alive
```

DisassociateMembers

Disassociates the Amazon GuardDuty member accounts that are specified by the account IDs from their master account.

Request Syntax

```
1 POST https://<endpoint>/detector/{detectorId}/member/disassociate
```

Body:

```
1 {
2     "accountIds": [
3         {
4             "accountId": "string"
5         }
6     ]
7 }
```

Request Parameters

detectorID
The unique ID of the detector of the GuardDuty account whose members you want to disassociate from the master account.
Type: String
Required: Yes

Request Parameters

The request accepts the following data in JSON format.

accountIds
A list of account IDs of the GuardDuty member accounts that you want to disassociate from the master account.
Type: Array of strings
Required: Yes
accountID
AWS account ID.
Type: String

Response Syntax

```
1 {
2     "unprocessedAccounts": [
3         {
4             "accountId": "string",
5             "result": "string"
6         }
7     ]
8 }
```

Response Elements

If the action is successful, the service sends back an HTTP 200 response.

The following data is returned in JSON format by the service.

unprocessedAccounts
A list of account ID and email address pairs of the AWS accounts that could not be processed.
Type: Array of strings
accountID
The ID of the AWS account that could not be processed.
Type: String
result
The reason why the AWS account could not be processed.
Type: String

Errors

If the action is not successful, the service sends back an HTTP error response code along with detailed error information.

InvalidInputException

The request is rejected. The current account cannot delete the specified member account ID because it is still associated with it.

HTTP Status Code: 200

InvalidInputException

The request is rejected. An invalid or out-of-range value is specified as an input parameter.

HTTP Status Code: 400

InvalidInputException

The request is rejected. The required query or path parameters are not specified.

HTTP Status Code: 400

InvalidInputException

The request is rejected. One or more input parameters have invalid values.

HTTP Status Code: 400

InvalidInputException

The request is rejected. The parameter `detectorId` has an invalid value.

HTTP Status Code: 400

NoSuchEntryException

The request is rejected. The input `detectorId` is not owned by the current account.

HTTP Status Code: 400

InternalException

Internal server error.

HTTP Status Code: 500

Example

Sample Request

```
1 POST /detector/26b092acdf3e60c625b69013f7488f7b/member/disassociate HTTP/1.1
2 Host: guardduty.us-west-2.amazonaws.com
3 Accept-Encoding: identity
4 Content-Length: 32
5 Authorization: AUTHPARAMS
6 X-Amz-Date: 20180209T215810Z
7 User-Agent: aws-cli/1.14.29 Python/2.7.9 Windows/8 botocore/1.8.33
8 {
9     "accountIds":[
10         "123456789012"
11     ]
12 }
```

Sample Response

```
1 HTTP/1.1 200 OK
2 Content-Type: application/json
3 Content-Length: 26
4 Date: Fri, 09 Feb 2018 21:58:11 GMT
5 x-amzn-RequestId: 51eb275c-0de4-11e8-bd33-c5cd21578c63
6 X-Amzn-Trace-Id: sampled=0;root=1-5a7e1973-693807dcdf14863bb877761c
7 X-Cache: Miss from cloudfront
8 Via: 1.1 e1fff2dee56e3b55796cc594a92413c0.cloudfront.net (CloudFront)
9 X-Amz-Cf-Id: E-zJ6yx-omadkYphY1mJTcfyXKjSFJsh38MFTh-pIiNLWdjqo5tLNw==
10 Connection: Keep-alive
11 {
12     "unprocessedAccounts":[
13
14     ]
15 }
```

GetDetector

Returns the properties of the Amazon GuardDuty detector that is specified by the detector ID.

Request Syntax

```
1 GET https://<endpoint>/detector/{detectorId}
```

Path Parameters

detectorId
The unique ID of the detector that you want to describe.
Type: String
Required: Yes

Response Syntax

```
1 {
2     "serviceRole": "string",
3     "status": "string",
4     "createdAt": "string",
5     "updatedAt": "string"
6 }
```

Response Elements

If the action is successful, the service sends back an HTTP 200 response.

The response is the following data in JSON format.

serviceRole
The service-linked role that grants GuardDuty access to the resources in the AWS account.
Type: String

status
The current status of the detector.
Type: String. Valid Values: ENABLED | DISABLED

createdAt
The time at which the detector was created.
Type: ISO 8601 string format: YYYY-MM-DDTHH:MM:SS.SSSZ or YYYY-MM-DDTHH:MM:SSZ depending on whether the value contains milliseconds.

updatedAt
The time at which detector was last updated.
Type: ISO 8601 string format: YYYY-MM-DDTHH:MM:SS.SSSZ or YYYY-MM-DDTHH:MM:SSZ depending on whether the value contains milliseconds.

Errors

If the action is not successful, the service returns an HTTP error response code along with detailed error information.

InvalidInputException

The request is rejected. An invalid or out-of-range value is specified as an input parameter.

HTTP Status Code: 400

InvalidInputException

The request is rejected. The required query or path parameters are not specified.

HTTP Status Code: 400

InvalidInputException

The request is rejected. One or more input parameters have invalid values.

HTTP Status Code: 400

InvalidInputException

The request is rejected. The parameter `detectorId` has an invalid value.

HTTP Status Code: 400

NoSuchEntityException

The request is rejected. The input `detectorId` is not owned by the current account.

HTTP Status Code: 400

NoSuchEntityException

Internal server error.

HTTP Status Code: 500

Example

Sample Request

```
1 GET /detector/12abc34d567e8fa901bc2d34e56789f0 HTTP/1.1
2 Host: guardduty.us-west-2.amazonaws.com
3 Accept-Encoding: identity
4 Authorization: AUTHPARAMS
5 X-Amz-Date: 20180123T220712Z
6 User-Agent: aws-cli/1.14.29 Python/2.7.9 Windows/8 botocore/1.8.33
```

Sample Response

```
1 HTTP/1.1 200 OK
2 Content-Type: application/json
3 Content-Length: 220
4 Date: Tue, 23 Jan 2018 22:07:13 GMT
5 x-amzn-RequestId: c3cfdfa5-0089-11e8-a4e2-07af7075b461
6 X-Amzn-Trace-Id: sampled=0;root=1-5a67b211-9b4ca2adcf4a8bc402a66eac
7 X-Cache: Miss from cloudfront
8 Via: 1.1 fe951a27fbed2178f4268c584d282a1d.cloudfront.net (CloudFront)
9 X-Amz-Cf-Id: VcRcgzIE3MRFumWYKiXjXsoaY2GJSPSo7Q4eSDp7dNquhfxzrZgbgA==
10 Connection: Keep-alive
11 {
12     "status":"DISABLED",
13     "createdAt":"2018-01-23T21:53:32.815Z",
14     "updatedAt":"2018-01-23T21:53:32.815Z",
15     "serviceRole":"arn:aws:iam::123456789012:role/aws-service-role/guardduty.amazonaws.com/
        AWSServiceRoleForAmazonGuardDuty"
```

16 }

GetFilter

Returns the details of the filter specified by the filter name.

Request Syntax

```
1 GET https://<endpoint>/detector/{detectorId}/filter/<filterName>
```

Path Parameters

detectorId
The detector ID that specifies the GuardDuty service where you want to list the details of the specified filter.
Type: String
Required: Yes

filterName
The name of the filter whose details you want to get.
Type: String
Required: Yes

Response Syntax

```
1  {
2          "name": "string",
3          "description": "string",
4          "findingCriteria":  [
5              "criterion": {
6                  "<field>": {
7                      "gt": "integer",
8                      "gte": "integer",
9                      "lt": "integer",
10                     "lte": "integer",
11                     "eq": [
12                         "string"
13                     ],
14                     "neq": [
15                         "string"
16                     ]
17                 }
18             }
19         ],
20         "action": "[NOOP|ARCHIVE]",
21         "rank": "integer"
22 }
```

Response Elements

If the action is successful, the service sends back an HTTP 200 response.

The following data is returned in JSON format by the service.

filter
The returned details of the filter.

name

The name of the filter.

Type: String

description

The description of the filter.

Type: String

findingCriteria

Represents the criteria to be used in the filter for querying findings.

Type: FindingCriteria

Required: No

You can only use the following attributes to query findings:

- accountId

- id

- region

- resource.instanceDetails.instanceId

- resource.resourceType

- service.archived **Note**

  When this attribute is set to TRUE, only archived findings are listed. When it's set to FALSE, only unarchived findings are listed. When this attribute is not set, all existing findings are listed.

- service.action.networkConnectionAction.blocked

- service.action.networkConnectionAction.connectionDirection

- service.action.networkConnectionAction.localPortDetails.port

- service.action.networkConnectionAction.protocol

- service.action.networkConnectionAction.remoteIpDetails.ipAddressV4

- service.action.networkConnectionAction.remotePortDetails.port

- service.action.actionType

- service.additionalInfo.threatListName

- severity

- type

- updatedAt

  Type: ISO 8601 string format: YYYY-MM-DDTHH:MM:SS.SSSZ or YYYY-MM-DDTHH:MM:SSZ depending on whether the value contains milliseconds.
  Gt

  Represents the "greater than" condition to be applied to a single field when querying for findings.

  Required: No

  Gte

  Represents the "greater than equal" condition to be applied to a single field when querying for findings.

  Required: No

  Lt

  Represents the "less than" condition to be applied to a single field when querying for findings.

  Required: No

  Lte

  Represents the "less than equal" condition to be applied to a single field when querying for findings.

  Required: No

  Eq

Represents the "equal to" condition to be applied to a single field when querying for findings.
Required: No
Neq
Represents the "not equal to" condition to be applied to a single field when querying for findings.
Required: No
rank
Specifies the position of the filter in the list of current filters. Also specifies the order in which this filter is applied to the findings.
Type: Integer
action
Specifies the action that is to be applied to the findings that match the filter.

Errors

If the action is not successful, the service sends back an HTTP error response code along with detailed error information.

InvalidInputException

The request is rejected. An invalid or out-of-range value is specified as an input parameter.

HTTP Status Code: 400

InvalidInputException

The request is rejected. The required query or path parameters are not specified.

HTTP Status Code: 400

InvalidInputException

The request is rejected. One or more input parameters have invalid values.

HTTP Status Code: 400

InvalidInputException

The request is rejected. The parameter `detectorId` has an invalid value.

HTTP Status Code: 400

InvalidInputException

The request is rejected. The parameter `name` has an invalid value.

HTTP Status Code: 400

NoSuchEntityException

The request is rejected. The input detectorId is not owned by the current account.

HTTP Status Code: 400

NoSuchEntityException

The request is rejected. The input `name` is not owned by the current account.

HTTP Status Code: 400

InternalException

Internal server error.

HTTP Status Code: 500

GetFindings

Describes Amazon GuardDuty findings that are specified by finding IDs.

Request Syntax

```
1 POST https://<endpoint>/detector/{detectorId}/findings/get
```

```
1 {
2     "findingIds": [
3         "string"
4     ],
5     "sortCriteria": {
6         "attributeName": "string",
7         "orderBy": "[ASC|DESC]"
8     }
9 }
```

Path Parameters

detectorId
The detector ID that specifies the GuardDuty service whose findings you want to describe.
Type: String
Required: Yes

Request Parameters

The request accepts the following data in JSON format.

findingIds
The IDs of the findings that you want to describe.
Type: array of Strings. Minimum number of 0 items. Maximum number of 50 items.
Required: Yes

sortCriteria
Represents the criteria used to query for sorting.
Type: sortCriteria
Required: No
attributeName
An attribute in a finding that can be queried.
You can only use the following attributes to sort findings:

- accountId

- severity

- confidence

- type

- service.eventFirstSeen

- service.eventLastSeen

- createdAt

  Type: ISO 8601 string format: YYYY-MM-DDTHH:MM:SS.SSSZ or YYYY-MM-DDTHH:MM:SSZ depending on whether the value contains milliseconds.

- updatedAt

  Type: ISO 8601 string format: YYYY-MM-DDTHH:MM:SS.SSSZ or YYYY-MM-DDTHH:MM:SSZ depending on whether the value contains milliseconds.

- service.action.networkConnectionAction.remoteIpDetails.ipAddressV4

- resource.instanceDetails.instanceId

- service.action.networkConnectionAction.localPortDetails.port

- service.action.networkConnectionAction.remotePortDetails.port

- service.action.networkConnectionAction.remoteIpDetails.country.countryName

- service.action.networkConnectionAction.protocol, service.action.awsApiCallAction.api

- service.action.awsApiCallAction.serviceName

- service.action.networkConnectionAction.blocked

- service.count Type: String
  orderBy
  The order of the sorting request.
  Type: String. Valid values: [ASC | DESC]

Response Syntax

```
1  {
2      "findings": [
3          {
4              "schemaVersion": "string",
5              "accountId": "string",
6              "region": "string",
7              "partition": "string",
8              "id": "string",
9              "arn": "string",
10             "type": "string",
11             "resource": {
12                 "resourceType": "string",
13                 "instanceDetails": {
14                     "iamInstanceProfile": {
15                         "arn": "string",
16                         "id": "string"
17                     },
18                     "imageId": "string",
19                     "instanceId": "string",
20                     "instanceState": "string",
21                     "instanceType": "string",
22                     "launchTime": "string",
23                     "networkInterfaces": [
24                         {
25                             "publicDnsName": "string",
26                             "publicIp": "string",
27                             "securityGroups": [
```

```
28                            {
29                                "groupName": "string",
30                                "groupId": "string"
31                            }
32                        ],
33                        "ipv6Addresses": [
34                            "string"
35                        ],
36                        "privateDnsName": "string",
37                        "privateIpAddress": "string",
38                        "privateIpAddresses": [
39                            {
40                                "privateDnsName": "string",
41                                "privateIpAddress": "string"
42                            }
43                        ],
44                        "subnetId": "string",
45                        "vpcId": "string"
46                    }
47                ],
48                "availabilityZone": "string",
49                "platform": "string",
50                "productCodes": [
51                    {
52                        "code": "string",
53                        "productType": "string"
54                    }
55                ],
56                "tags": [
57                    {
58                        "key": "string",
59                        "value": "string"
60                    }
61                ]
62            },
63            "accessKeyDetails": {
64                "accessKeyId": "string",
65                "principalId": "string",
66                "userType": "string",
67                "userName": "string"
68            }
69        },
70        "service": {
71            "serviceName": "string",
72            "detectorId": "string",
73            "action": {
74                "actionType": "string",
75                "networkConnectionAction": {
76                    "connectionDirection": "string",
77                    "remoteIpDetails": {
78                        "ipAddressV4": "string",
79                        "organization": {
80                            "asn": "string",
81                            "asnOrg": "string",
```

```
 82                    "isp": "string",
 83                    "org": "string"
 84               },
 85               "country": {
 86                    "countryCode": "string",
 87                    "countryName": "string"
 88               },
 89               "city": {
 90                    "cityName": "string"
 91               },
 92               "geoLocation": {
 93                    "lat": "double",
 94                    "lon": "double"
 95               }
 96          },
 97          "remotePortDetails": {
 98               "port": "integer",
 99               "portName": "string"
100          },
101          "localPortDetails": {
102               "port": "integer",
103               "portName": "string"
104          },
105          "protocol": "string",
106          "blocked": "boolean"
107     },
108     "awsApiCallAction": {
109          "api": "string",
110          "serviceName": "string",
111          "callerType": "string",
112          "remoteIpDetails": {
113               "ipAddressV4": "string",
114               "organization": {
115                    "asn": "string",
116                    "asnOrg": "string",
117                    "isp": "string",
118                    "org": "string"
119               },
120               "country": {
121                    "countryCode": "string",
122                    "countryName": "string"
123               },
124               "city": {
125                    "cityName": "string"
126               },
127               "geoLocation": {
128                    "lat": "double",
129                    "lon": "double"
130               }
131          },
132          "domainDetails": {
133               "domain": "string"
134          }
135     },
```

```
136              "dnsRequestAction": {
137                  "domain": "string"
138              }
139          },
140          "resourceRole": "string",
141          "additionalInfo": {},
142          "eventFirstSeen": "string",
143          "eventLastSeen": "string",
144          "userFeedback": "string",
145          "archived": "boolean",
146          "count": "string"
147      },
148      "title": "string",
149      "description": "string",
150      "severity": "float",
151      "confidence": "float",
152      "createdAt": "string",
153      "updatedAt": "string"
154   }
155   ]
156 }
```

Response Elements

If the action is successful, the service sends back an HTTP 200 response.

The following data is returned in JSON format by the service.

findings
A list of returned findings.
Type: Array

schemaVersion
A finding's schema version.
Type: String

accountId
The AWS account ID where the activity occurred that prompted GuardDuty to generate a finding.
Type: String

region
The AWS Region where the activity occurred that prompted GuardDuty to generate a finding.
Type: String

partition
The AWS resource partition where the activity occurred that prompted GuardDuty to generate a finding.
Type: String

id
The finding ID.
Type: String

arn
The finding ARN.
Type: String

type
The finding type.
Type: String

resource
The AWS resource that is associated with the activity that prompted GuardDuty to generate a finding.
Type: Resource

type

The type of the AWS resource.

Type: String

instanceDetails

The information about the EC2 instance that is associated with the activity that prompted GuardDuty to generate a finding.

Type: InstanceDetails

iamInstanceProfile

The profile information of the EC2 instance.

Type: IamInstanceProfile

arn

The AWS EC2 instance profile ARN.

Type: String

id

The AWS EC2 instance profile ID.

Type: String

imageId

The image ID of the EC2 instance.

Type: String

instanceId

The ID of the EC2 instance.

Type: String

instanceState

The state of the EC2 instance.

Type: String

instanceType

The type of the EC2 instance.

Type: String

launchTime

The launch time of the EC2 instance.

Type: String

networkInterfaces

The network interface information of the EC2 instance.

Type: NetworkInterfaces

publicDnsName

The public DNS name of the EC2 instance.

Type: String

publicIp

The public IP address of the EC2 instance.

Type: String

securityGroups

The security groups that are associated with the EC2 instance.

Type: SecurityGroups

groupName

The security group name of the EC2 instance.

Type: String

groupId

The security group ID of the EC2 instance.

Type: String

Ipv6Addresses

The IpV6 address information of the EC2 instance.

Type: Array of strings

privateDnsName

The private DNS name of the EC2 instance.

Type: String

privateIpAddress

The private IP address of the EC2 instance.

Type: String

privateIpAddresses

Other private IP address information of the EC2 instance.

Type: PrivateIPAddresses

privateDnsName

The private DNS name information that corresponds to the private IP address.

Type: String

privateIpAddress

The Inet private IP address.

Type: String

subnetId

The subnet ID.

Type: String

vpcId

The VPC ID.

Type: String

availabilityZone

The Availability Zone of the EC2 instance.

Type: String

platform

The platform of the EC2 instance.

Type: String

productCodes

The product code of the EC2 instance.

Type: List of ProductCodes

code

The product code information.

Type: String

productType

The product code type.

Type: String

tags

The tags of the EC2 instance.

Type: Tags

key

The EC2 instance tag key.

Type: String

value

The EC2 instance tag value.

Type: String

accessKeyDetails

The IAM access key details (IAM user information) of a user that engaged in the activity that prompted GuardDuty to generate a finding.

Type: AccessKeyDetails

accessKeyId

The access key ID of the user.

Type: String

principalId

The principal ID of the user.

Type: String

userType

The type of the user.

Type: String

userName

The name of the user.

Type: String

service

Additional information assigned to the generated finding by GuardDuty.

Type: Service

serviceName

The name of the AWS service (GuardDuty) that generated a finding.

Type: String

detectorId

The detector ID for the GuardDuty service.

Type: String

action

Information about the activity that is described in a finding.

Type: Action

actionType

The activity type of the GuardDuty finding.

Type: String

networkConnectionAction

Information about the `NETWORK_CONNECTION` action that is described in this finding.

Type: NetworkConnectionAction

connectionDirection

The network connection direction.

Type: String

remoteIpDetails

The remote IP information of the connection.

Type: RemoteIpDetails

ipAddressV4

The IPV4 remote address of the connection.

Type: String

organization

The ISP organization information of the remote IP address.

Type: Organization

asn

The autonomous system number of the internet provider of the remote IP address.

Type: String

asnOrg

The organization that registered this ASN.

Type: String

isp

The ISP information for the internet provider.

Type: String

org

The name of the internet provider.

Type: String

country

The country information of the remote IP address.

Type: Country

countryName

The city name of the remote IP address.

Type: String

countryCode

The country code of the remote IP address.

Type: String

city

The city information of the remote IP address.

Type: City

cityName

The city name of the remote IP address.

Type: String

geoLocation

The location information of the remote IP address.

Type: GeoLocation

lon

The longitude information of the remote IP address.

Type: Double

lat

The latitude information of the remote IP address.

Type: Double

remotePortDetails

The remote port information of the connection.

Type: RemotePortDetails

port

The port number of the remote connection.

Type: Integer

portName

The port name of the remote connection.

Type: String

localPortDetails

The local port information of the connection.

Type: LocalPortDetails

port

The port number of the local connection.

Type: Integer

portName

The port name of the local connection.

Type: String

protocol

The network connection protocol.

Type: String

blocked

The network connection blocked information.

Type: Boolean

awsApiCallAction

Information about the `AWS_API_CALL` action that is described in this finding.

Type: AwsApiCallAction

api

The AWS API name.

Type: String

serviceName

The AWS service name whose API was invoked.

Type: String

callerType

The AWS API caller type.

Type: String

remoteIpDetails

The remote IP information of the connection.

Type: RemoteIpDetails

ipAddressV4

The IPV4 remote address of the connection.

Type: String

organization

The ISP organization information of the remote IP address.

Type: Organization

asn

The autonomous system number of the internet provider.

Type: String

asnOrg

The organization that registered this ASN.

Type: String

isp

The ISP information for the internet provider.

Type: String

org

The name of the internet provider.

Type: String

country

The country information of the remote IP address.

Type: Country

countryName

The city name of the remote IP address.

Type: String

countryCode

The country code of the remote IP address.

Type: String

city

The city information of the remote IP address.

Type: City

cityName

The city name of the remote IP address.

Type: String

geoLocation

The location information of the remote IP address.

Type: GeoLocation

lon

The longitude information of the remote IP address.

Type: Double

lat

The latitude information of the remote IP address.

Type: Double

domainDetails

The domain information for the AWS API call.

Type: DomainDetails

domain

The domain information for the AWS API call.

Type: String

dnsRequestAction

Information about the `DNS_REQUEST` action that is described in this finding.

Type: DnsRequestAction

domain

Domain information for the DNS request.

Type: String

resourceRole

Resource role information for this finding.

Type: String

additionalInfo

The list of additional information for this finding.

eventFirstSeen

The first seen timestamp of the activity that prompted GuardDuty to generate this finding.

Type: ISO 8601 string format: YYYY-MM-DDTHH:MM:SS.SSSZ or YYYY-MM-DDTHH:MM:SSZ depending on whether the value contains milliseconds.

eventLastSeen

The last seen timestamp of the activity that prompted GuardDuty to generate this finding.

Type: ISO 8601 string format: YYYY-MM-DDTHH:MM:SS.SSSZ or YYYY-MM-DDTHH:MM:SSZ depending on whether the value contains milliseconds.

userFeedback

Feedback provided by a user about the finding.

Type: String

archived

Specifies whether this finding is archived.

Type: Boolean

count

The total count of the occurrences of this finding type.

Type: String

title

The title of a finding.

Type: String

description

The description of a finding.

Type: String

severity

The severity of a finding.

Type: float

confidence

The confidence level of a finding.

Type: float

createdAt

The time stamp at which a finding was generated.

Type: ISO 8601 string format: YYYY-MM-DDTHH:MM:SS.SSSZ or YYYY-MM-DDTHH:MM:SSZ depending on whether the value contains milliseconds.

updatedAt

The time stamp at which a finding was last updated.

Type: ISO 8601 string format: YYYY-MM-DDTHH:MM:SS.SSSZ or YYYY-MM-DDTHH:MM:SSZ depending on whether the value contains milliseconds.

Errors

If the action is not successful, the service sends back an HTTP error response code along with detailed error information.

InvalidInputException

The request is rejected. An invalid or out-of-range value is specified as an input parameter.

HTTP Status Code: 400

InvalidInputException

The request is rejected. The required query or path parameters are not specified.

HTTP Status Code: 400

InvalidInputException

The request is rejected. One or more input parameters have invalid values.

HTTP Status Code: 400

InvalidInputException

The request is rejected. The parameter `detectorId` has an invalid value.

HTTP Status Code: 400

InvalidInputException

The request is rejected. The parameter `findingCriteria` has an invalid value.

HTTP Status Code: 400

InvalidInputException

The request is rejected. An invalid finding statistic type is specified.

HTTP Status Code: 400

NoSuchEntityException

The request is rejected. The input `detectorId` is not owned by the current account.

HTTP Status Code: 400

InternalException

Internal server error.

HTTP Status Code: 500

Example

Sample Request

```
1 POST /detector/c6b0be64463ff852400d8ae5b2353866/findings/get HTTP/1.1
2 Host: guardduty.us-west-2.amazonaws.com
3 Accept-Encoding: identity
4 Content-Length: 52
5 Authorization: AUTHPARAMS
6 X-Amz-Date: 20180209T232830Z
7 User-Agent: aws-cli/1.14.29 Python/2.7.9 Windows/8 botocore/1.8.33
8 {
9    "findingIds":[
10       "9cb0be64df8ba1df249c45eb8a0bf584"
11    ]
12 }
```

Sample Response

```
1 HTTP/1.1 200 OK
2 Content-Type: application/json
3 Content-Length: 3290
4 Date: Fri, 09 Feb 2018 23:28:31 GMT
```

```
 5 x-amzn-RequestId: f0876f86-0df0-11e8-900a-559d93fe6c5b
 6 X-Amzn-Trace-Id: sampled=0;root=1-5a7e2e9f-d77815a82381c4f592d527bd
 7 X-Cache: Miss from cloudfront
 8 Via: 1.1 39f9e0f028321e95b5ebd1cd55661fd6.cloudfront.net (CloudFront)
 9 X-Amz-Cf-Id: FWbQHHuN2DoUqO9CxoJfxvOMhjH9v2t9uPRf_d_uIBRD7tEXvhmINg==
10 Connection: Keep-alive
11 {
12     "findings":[
13         {
14             "schemaVersion":"2.0",
15             "accountId":"123456789012",
16             "region":"us-west-2",
17             "partition":"aws",
18             "id":"9cb0be64df8ba1df249c45eb8a0bf584",
19             "arn":"arn:aws:guardduty:us-west-2:123456789012:detector/
                    c6b0be64463ff852400d8ae5b2353866/finding/9cb0be64df8ba1df249c45eb8a0bf584",
20             "type":"UnauthorizedAccess:EC2/RDPBruteForce",
21             "resource":{
22                 "resourceType":"Instance",
23                 "instanceDetails":{
24                     "instanceId":"i-99999999",
25                     "instanceType":"m3.xlarge",
26                     "launchTime":"2016-08-02T02:05:06Z",
27                     "platform":null,
28                     "productCodes":[
29                         {
30                             "productCodeId":"GeneratedFindingProductCodeId",
31                             "productCodeType":"GeneratedFindingProductCodeType"
32                         }
33                     ],
34                     "iamInstanceProfile":{
35                         "arn":"GeneratedFindingInstanceProfileArn",
36                         "id":"GeneratedFindingInstanceProfileId"
37                     },
38                     "networkInterfaces":[
39                         {
40                             "ipv6Addresses":[
41
42                             ],
43                             "privateDnsName":"GeneratedFindingPrivateDnsName",
44                             "privateIpAddress":"10.0.0.1",
45                             "privateIpAddresses":[
46                                 {
47                                     "privateDnsName":"GeneratedFindingPrivateName",
48                                     "privateIpAddress":"10.0.0.1"
49                                 }
50                             ],
51                             "subnetId":"GeneratedFindingSubnetId",
52                             "vpcId":"GeneratedFindingVPCId",
53                             "securityGroups":[
54                                 {
55                                     "groupName":"GeneratedFindingSecurityGroupName",
56                                     "groupId":"GeneratedFindingSecurityId"
57                                 }
```

```
58              ],
59              "publicDnsName":"GeneratedFindingPublicDNSName",
60              "publicIp":"198.51.100.0"
61            }
62          ],
63          "tags":[
64            {
65              "key":"GeneratedFindingInstaceTag1",
66              "value":"GeneratedFindingInstaceValue1"
67            },
68            {
69              "key":"GeneratedFindingInstaceTag2",
70              "value":"GeneratedFindingInstaceTagValue2"
71            },
72            {
73              "key":"GeneratedFindingInstaceTag3",
74              "value":"GeneratedFindingInstaceTagValue3"
75            },
76            {
77              "key":"GeneratedFindingInstaceTag4",
78              "value":"GeneratedFindingInstaceTagValue4"
79            },
80            {
81              "key":"GeneratedFindingInstaceTag5",
82              "value":"GeneratedFindingInstaceTagValue5"
83            },
84            {
85              "key":"GeneratedFindingInstaceTag6",
86              "value":"GeneratedFindingInstaceTagValue6"
87            },
88            {
89              "key":"GeneratedFindingInstaceTag7",
90              "value":"GeneratedFindingInstaceTagValue7"
91            },
92            {
93              "key":"GeneratedFindingInstaceTag8",
94              "value":"GeneratedFindingInstaceTagValue8"
95            },
96            {
97              "key":"GeneratedFindingInstaceTag9",
98              "value":"GeneratedFindingInstaceTagValue9"
99            }
100         ],
101         "instanceState":"running",
102         "availabilityZone":"GeneratedFindingInstaceAvailabilityZone",
103         "imageId":"ami-99999999",
104         "imageDescription":"GeneratedFindingInstaceImageDescription"
105       }
106     },
107     "service":{
108       "serviceName":"guardduty",
109       "detectorId":"c6b0be64463ff852400d8ae5b2353866",
110       "action":{
111         "actionType":"NETWORK_CONNECTION",
```

```
112                     "networkConnectionAction":{
113                         "connectionDirection":"INBOUND",
114                         "remoteIpDetails":{
115                             "ipAddressV4":"198.51.100.0",
116                             "organization":{
117                                 "asn":"-1",
118                                 "asnOrg":"GeneratedFindingASNOrg",
119                                 "isp":"GeneratedFindingISP",
120                                 "org":"GeneratedFindingORG"
121                             },
122                             "country":{
123                                 "countryName":"GeneratedFindingCountryName"
124                             },
125                             "city":{
126                                 "cityName":"GeneratedFindingCityName"
127                             },
128                             "geoLocation":{
129                                 "lat":0,
130                                 "lon":0
131                             }
132                         },
133                         "remotePortDetails":{
134                             "port":1067,
135                             "portName":"Unknown"
136                         },
137                         "localPortDetails":{
138                             "port":3389,
139                             "portName":"RDP"
140                         },
141                         "protocol":"TCP",
142                         "blocked":false
143                     }
144                 },
145                 "resourceRole":"TARGET",
146                 "additionalInfo":{
147                     "sample":true
148                 },
149                 "eventFirstSeen":"2018-02-09T22:57:31.927Z",
150                 "eventLastSeen":"2018-02-09T22:57:31.927Z",
151                 "archived":false,
152                 "count":1,
153                 "userFeedback":"NOT_USEFUL"
154             },
155             "severity":2,
156             "createdAt":"2018-02-09T22:57:31.927Z",
157             "updatedAt":"2018-02-09T22:57:31.927Z",
158             "title":"198.51.100.0 is performing RDP brute force attacks against i-99999999.",
159             "description":"198.51.100.0 is performing RDP brute force attacks against i-99999999.
                    Brute force attacks are used to gain unauthorized access to your instance by
                    guessing the RDP password."
160         }
161     ]
162 }
```

GetFindingsStatistics

Lists the statistics for the findings for the specified detector ID.

Request Syntax

```
1 POST https://<endpoint>/detector/{detectorId}/findings/statistics
```

Body:

```
1  {
2      "findingCriteria": {
3          "criterion": {
4              "<field>": {
5                  "Gt": "integer",
6                  "Gte": "integer",
7                  "Lt": "integer",
8                  "Lte": "integer",
9                  "Eq": [
10                     "string"
11                 ],
12                 "Neq": [
13                     "string"
14                 ]
15             }
16         }
17     }
18     "findingStatisticTypes": {
19         "findingStatisticType": "[COUNT_BY_SEVERITY]"
20     }
21
22 }
```

Path Parameters

detectorId
The ID of the detector whose findings' statistics you want to get.
Required: Yes

Request Parameters

The request accepts the following data in JSON format.

findingCriteria
The criteria that is used for querying findings.
Type: FindingCriteria
Required: No
Gt
Represents the "greater than" condition to be applied to a single field when querying for findings.
Required: No
Gte
Represents the "greater than equal" condition to be applied to a single field when querying for findings.
Required: No

Lt

Represents the "less than" condition to be applied to a single field when querying for findings.
Required: No

Lte

Represents the "less than equal" condition to be applied to a single field when querying for findings.
Required: No

Eq

Represents the "equal to" condition to be applied to a single field when querying for findings.
Required: No

Neq

Represents the "not equal to" condition to be applied to a single field when querying for findings.
Required: No

findingStatisticTypes

The list of the finding statistics.
Required: Yes
Type: Array of strings. Minimum items 1. Maximum items 10.

FindingStatisticType

The types of finding statistics.
Type: String. Valid values: [COUNT_BY_SEVERITY]

Response Syntax

```
1 {
2     "findingStatistics": [
3         {
4             "countBySeverity": "integer",
5         }
6     ]
7 }
```

Response Elements

If the action is successful, the service sends back an HTTP 200 response.

The following data is returned in JSON format by the service.

findingStatistics

Represents a map of severity or count statistics for a set of findings.
Type: Integer

Errors

If the action is not successful, the service sends back an HTTP error response code along with detailed error information.

InvalidInputException

The request is rejected. An invalid or out-of-range value is specified as an input parameter.

HTTP Status Code: 400

InvalidInputException

The request is rejected. The required query or path parameters are not specified.

HTTP Status Code: 400

134

InvalidInputException

The request is rejected. One or more input parameters have invalid values.

HTTP Status Code: 400

InvalidInputException

The request is rejected. The parameter `detectorId` has an invalid value.

HTTP Status Code: 400

InvalidInputException

The request is rejected. The parameter `findingCriteria` has an invalid value.

HTTP Status Code: 400

InvalidInputException

The request is rejected. An invalid finding statistic type is specified.

HTTP Status Code: 400

NoSuchEntityException

The request is rejected. The input `detectorId` is not owned by the current account.

HTTP Status Code: 400

InternalException

Internal server error.

HTTP Status Code: 500

Example

Sample Request

```
1 POST /detector/26b092acdf3e60c625b69013f7488f7b/findings/statistics HTTP/1.1
2 Host: guardduty.us-west-2.amazonaws.com
3 Accept-Encoding: identity
4 Content-Length: 48
5 Authorization: AUTHPARAMS
6 X-Amz-Date: 20180209T225034Z
7 User-Agent: aws-cli/1.14.29 Python/2.7.9 Windows/8 botocore/1.8.33
8 {
9     "findingStatisticTypes":[
10        "COUNT_BY_SEVERITY"
11    ]
12 }
```

Sample Response

```
1 HTTP/1.1 200 OK
2 Content-Type: application/json
3 Content-Length: 52
4 Date: Fri, 09 Feb 2018 22:50:36 GMT
5 x-amzn-RequestId: a44aa11e-0deb-11e8-8707-25a841979d1b
6 X-Amzn-Trace-Id: sampled=0;root=1-5a7e25bb-554e828c4c44bf219cac7cff
7 X-Cache: Miss from cloudfront
8 Via: 1.1 e6ed0c52befaa18f2fc5054cafda6db7.cloudfront.net (CloudFront)
```

```
 9 X-Amz-Cf-Id: zXlGhggMhDACYc_qMeJLEgyaxPSaVA_vjzdsvaV-bXoAsccJGk_rzw==
10 Connection: Keep-alive
11 {
12     "findingStatistics":{
13         "countBySeverity":{
14             "2.0":45
15         }
16     }
17 }
```

GetInvitationsCount

Returns the count of all Amazon GuardDuty membership invitations that were sent to the current member account, not including the currently accepted invitation.

Request Syntax

```
1 GET https://<endpoint>/invitation/count
```

Response Syntax

```
1 {
2     "invitationsCount": "integer"
3 }
```

Response Elements

If the action is successful, the service sends back an HTTP 200 response.

The following data is returned in JSON format by the service.

invitationsCount
The number of all membership invitations sent to this GuardDuty member account, not including the currently accepted invitation.
Type: Integer

Errors

If the action is not successful, the service sends back an HTTP error response code along with detailed error information.

InvalidInputException

The request is rejected. An invalid or out-of-range value is specified as an input parameter.

HTTP Status Code: 400

InvalidInputException

The request is rejected. The required query or path parameters are not specified.

HTTP Status Code: 400

InvalidInputException

The request is rejected. One or more input parameters have invalid values.

HTTP Status Code: 400

InternalException

Internal server error.

HTTP Status Code: 500

Example

Sample Request

```
1 GET /invitation/count HTTP/1.1
2 Host: guardduty.us-west-2.amazonaws.com
3 Accept-Encoding: identity
4 Authorization: AUTHPARAMS
5 X-Amz-Date: 20180125T204945Z
6 User-Agent: aws-cli/1.14.29 Python/2.7.9 Windows/8 botocore/1.8.33
```

Sample Response

```
1 HTTP/1.1 200 OK
2 Content-Type: application/json
3 Content-Length: 22
4 Date: Thu, 25 Jan 2018 20:49:46 GMT
5 x-amzn-RequestId: 471e2f10-0211-11e8-ae9e-81995a5809d1
6 X-Amzn-Trace-Id: sampled=0;root=1-5a6a42ea-b7e4e135162fc10fffc6ed8b
7 X-Cache: Miss from cloudfront
8 Via: 1.1 452a6d5a60db801bab9900e11681a635.cloudfront.net (CloudFront)
9 X-Amz-Cf-Id: 2VlLvf233bVGY4yOB5rRATpTMVmyNDnOK5pgwA_OMugdypwnYMvpcQ==
10 Connection: Keep-alive
11 {
12     "invitationsCount":1
13 }
```

GetIPSet

Returns the properties of the IPSet that is specified by the IPSet ID.

Important
If a user from a member account runs this API, the response contains the IPSets uploaded by the master account. Currently in GuardDuty, users from member accounts CANNOT upload and further manage IPSets. IPSets that are uploaded by the master account are imposed on GuardDuty functionality in its member accounts. For more information, see Managing AWS Accounts in Amazon GuardDuty.

Request Syntax

```
1 GET https://<endpoint>/detector/{detectorId}/ipset/{ipSetId}
```

Body:

```
1 detectorId : "string"
2 ipSetId : "string"
```

Path Parameters

The request accepts the following data in JSON format.

detectorId
The detector ID that specifies the GuardDuty service whose IPSet properties you want to return.
Type: String
Required: Yes

ipSetId
The unique ID that specifies the IPSet whose properties you want to return.
Type: String
Required: Yes

Response Syntax

```
1 {
2     "name": "string",
3     "location": "string",
4     "format": "[TXT|STIX|OTX_CSV|ALIEN_VAULT|PROOF_POINT|FIRE_EYE]",
5     "status": "[INACTIVE|ACTIVATING|ACTIVE|DEACTIVATING|ERROR|DELETE_PENDING|DELETED]"
6 }
```

Response Elements

If the action is successful, the service sends back an HTTP 200 response.

The following data is returned in JSON format by the service.

name
The name of the IPSet.
Type: String

location
The URI of the file that contains the IPSet.
Type: String

format

The format of the file that contains the IPSet.

Type: String

Values : TXT | STIX | OTX_CSV | ALIEN_VAULT | PROOF_POINT | FIRE_EYE

status

The current status of the IPSet.

Valid values : INACTIVE | ACTIVATING | ACTIVE | DEACTIVATING | ERROR | DELETE_PENDING | DELETED

Type: String

Errors

If the action is not successful, the service returns an HTTP error response code along with detailed error information.

InvalidInputException

The request is rejected. An invalid or out-of-range value is specified as an input parameter.

HTTP Status Code: 400

InvalidInputException

The request is rejected. The required query or path parameters are not specified.

HTTP Status Code: 400

InvalidInputException

The request is rejected. One or more input parameters have invalid values.

HTTP Status Code: 400

InvalidInputException

The request is rejected. The parameter `detectorId` has an invalid value.

HTTP Status Code: 400

InvalidInputException

The request is rejected. An invalid `ipSetId` is specified.

HTTP Status Code: 400

NoSuchEntityException

The request is rejected. The input `detectorId` is not owned by the current account.

HTTP Status Code: 400

NoSuchEntityException

The request is rejected. An invalid `ipSetId` is specified.

HTTP Status Code: 400

InternalException

Internal server error.

HTTP Status Code: 500

Example

Sample Request

```
1 GET /detector/12abc34d567e8fa901bc2d34e56789f0/ipset/0cb0141ab9fbde177613ab9436212e90 HTTP/1.1
2 Host: guardduty.us-west-2.amazonaws.com
3 Accept-Encoding: identity
4 Authorization: AUTHPARAMS
5 X-Amz-Date: 20180124T001448Z
6 User-Agent: aws-cli/1.14.29 Python/2.7.9 Windows/8 botocore/1.8.33
```

Sample Response

```
1 HTTP/1.1 200 OK
2 Content-Type: application/json
3 Content-Length: 120
4 Date: Wed, 24 Jan 2018 00:14:49 GMT
5 x-amzn-RequestId: 976b1bdd-009b-11e8-adf3-757264fd7e81
6 X-Amzn-Trace-Id: sampled=0;root=1-5a67cff9-297a6d6a145fae5f3111b2d2
7 X-Cache: Miss from cloudfront
8 Via: 1.1 b2532cb29a55e8fe8106a4a9a9241592.cloudfront.net (CloudFront)
9 X-Amz-Cf-Id: Mibb3YLLQGISFxiVKVFAt6h_yPIRSC6F55XvF7SLOXeDQ_lNSIZdgw==
10 Connection: Keep-alive
11 {
12    "name":"ExampleIPSet",
13    "location":"https://s3.amazonaws.com/guarddutylists/exampleipset.txt",
14    "format":"TXT",
15    "status":"ACTIVE"
16 }
```

GetMasterAccount

Provides the details for the Amazon GuardDuty master account to the current member account.

Request Syntax

```
1 POST https://<endpoint>/detector/{detectorId}/master
```

Body:

```
1 detectorId : "string"
```

Path Parameters

The request accepts the following data in JSON format.

detectorID
The detector ID of the GuardDuty member account whose master account details you want to return.
Required: Yes
Type: String

Response Syntax

```
1  {
2      "master": [
3          {
4              "accountId": "string",
5              "invitationId": "string",
6              "invitedAt": "string",
7              "relationshipStatus": "string"
8          }
9      ]
10 }
```

Response Elements

If the action is successful, the service sends back an HTTP 200 response.

The following data is returned in JSON format by the service.

master
A list of details about the GuardDuty master account for the current member account.
Type: Array
accountId
The account ID of a GuardDuty master account.
Type: String
invitationId
The ID of the invitation sent to the member by the GuardDuty master account.
Type: String
invitedAt
The time stamp at which the invitation was sent to the member by the GuardDuty master account.
Type: String
relationshipStatus

The status of the relationship between the master account and the member account. Valid values: `STAGED` | `PENDING` | `DISABLED` | `ENABLED` | `REMOVED` | `RESIGNED` | `EMAILVERIFICATIONINPROGRESS` | `EMAILVERIFICATIONFAILED`

Type: String

Errors

If the action is not successful, the service sends back an HTTP error response code along with detailed error information.

InvalidInputException

The request is rejected. An invalid or out-of-range value is specified as an input parameter.

HTTP Status Code: 400

InvalidInputException

The request is rejected. The required query or path parameters are not specified.

HTTP Status Code: 400

InvalidInputException

The request is rejected. One or more input parameters have invalid values.

HTTP Status Code: 400

InvalidInputException

The request is rejected. The parameter `detectorId` has an invalid value.

HTTP Status Code: 400

NoSuchEntityException

The request is rejected. The input `detectorId` is not owned by the current account.

HTTP Status Code: 400

InternalException

Internal server error.

HTTP Status Code: 500

Example

Sample Request

```
1 GET /detector/12abc34d567e8fa901bc2d34e56789f0/master HTTP/1.1
2 Host: guardduty.us-west-2.amazonaws.com
3 Accept-Encoding: identity
4 Authorization: AUTHPARAMS
5 X-Amz-Date: 20180125T203733Z
6 User-Agent: aws-cli/1.14.29 Python/2.7.9 Windows/8 botocore/1.8.33
```

Sample Response

```
1 HTTP/1.1 200 OK
2 Content-Type: application/json
3 Content-Length: 161
4 Date: Thu, 25 Jan 2018 20:37:34 GMT
```

```
 5 x-amzn-RequestId: 93058ed0-020f-11e8-9ea1-377499f46311
 6 X-Amzn-Trace-Id: sampled=0;root=1-5a6a400e-0026139dc9abc8eaac805a22
 7 X-Cache: Miss from cloudfront
 8 Via: 1.1 6f1f8362062a31675dde3c27bc22f2ef.cloudfront.net (CloudFront)
 9 X-Amz-Cf-Id: NjMp1e2biYmUYjoe570CqcuDFXL3JO-_xB-8qad7moZvX-cl62iWBQ==
10 Connection: Keep-alive
11 {
12    "master":{
13       "accountId":"012345678901",
14       "invitationId":"84b097800250d17d1872b34c4daadcf5",
15       "invitedAt":"2018-01-25T20:26:25.825Z",
16       "relationshipStatus":"Monitored"
17    }
18 }
```

GetMembers

Returns the details on the Amazon GuardDuty member accounts that are specified by the account IDs.

Request Syntax

```
1 POST https://<endpoint>/detector/{detectorId}/member/get
```

Body:

```
1 {
2     "accountIds": [
3         {
4             "accountId": "string"
5         }
6     ]
7 }
```

Path Parameters

detectorID
The detector ID of the GuardDuty account on whose members you want to return the details.
Type: String
Required: Yes

Request Parameters

The request accepts the following data in JSON format.

accountIds
A list of account IDs for the GuardDuty member accounts on which you want to return the details.
Type: Array of strings
Required: Yes
accountID
The AWS account ID.
Type: String

Response Syntax

```
1 {
2     "members": [
3         {
4             "accountId": "string",
5             "detectorId": "string",
6             "email": "string",
7             "masterId": "string",
8             "relationshipStatus": "string",
9             "invitedAt": "string",
10            "updatedAt": "string"
11        }
12     ],
13     "unprocessedAccounts": [
```

```
14        {
15            "accountId": "string",
16            "result": "string"
17        }
18    ]
19 }
```

Response Elements

If the action is successful, the service sends back an HTTP 200 response.

The following data is returned in JSON format by the service.

members
A list of details about the GuardDuty member accounts.
Type: Array
accountId
The AWS account ID.
Type: String
detectorId
The unique ID of the GuardDuty member account.
Type: String
email
The email address of the GuardDuty member account.
Type: String
masterId
The account ID of the master GuardDuty for a member account.
Type: String
relationshipStatus
The status of the relationship between the member account and its master account. Valid values:
`CREATED` | `INVITED` | `DISABLED` | `ENABLED` | `REMOVED` | `RESIGNED` | `EMAILVERIFICATIONINPROGRESS` |
`EMAILVERIFICATIONFAILED`
Type: String
invitedAt
Time stamp at which the member account was invited to GuardDuty.
Type: ISO 8601 string format: YYYY-MM-DDTHH:MM:SS.SSSZ or YYYY-MM-DDTHH:MM:SSZ depending on whether the value contains milliseconds.
updatedAt
Time stamp at which this member account was updated.
Type: ISO 8601 string format: YYYY-MM-DDTHH:MM:SS.SSSZ or YYYY-MM-DDTHH:MM:SSZ depending on whether the value contains milliseconds.

unprocessedAccounts
A list of account ID and email address pairs of the AWS accounts that could not be processed.
Type: Array of strings
accountID
The ID of the AWS account that could not be processed.
Type: String
result
The reason why the AWS account could not be processed.
Type: String

Errors

If the action is not successful, the service sends back an HTTP error response code along with detailed error information.

InvalidInputException

The request is rejected. An invalid or out-of-range value is specified as an input parameter.

HTTP Status Code: 400

InvalidInputException

The request is rejected. The required query or path parameters are not specified.

HTTP Status Code: 400

InvalidInputException

The request is rejected. One or more input parameters have invalid values.

HTTP Status Code: 400

InvalidInputException

The request is rejected. The parameter `detectorId` has an invalid value.

HTTP Status Code: 400

NoSuchEntityException

The request is rejected. The input `detectorId` is not owned by the current account.

HTTP Status Code: 400

InternalException

Internal server error.

HTTP Status Code: 500

Example

Sample Request

```
1 POST /detector/26b092acdf3e60c625b69013f7488f7b/member/get HTTP/1.1
2 Host: guardduty.us-west-2.amazonaws.com
3 Accept-Encoding: identity
4 Content-Length: 32
5 Authorization: AUTHPARAMS
6 X-Amz-Date: 20180209T213609Z
7 User-Agent: aws-cli/1.14.29 Python/2.7.9 Windows/8 botocore/1.8.33
8 {
9     "accountIds":[
10         "123456789012"
11     ]
12 }
```

Sample Response

```
1 HTTP/1.1 200 OK
2 Content-Type: application/json
3 Content-Length: 283
4 Date: Fri, 09 Feb 2018 21:36:10 GMT
```

```
 5  x-amzn-RequestId: 3e768f7b-0de1-11e8-afbe-2bd59a045a01
 6  X-Amzn-Trace-Id: sampled=0;root=1-5a7e144a-24c5171e766097b2c56c3822
 7  X-Cache: Miss from cloudfront
 8  Via: 1.1 27a783405519f49942e72a6ed75f783f.cloudfront.net (CloudFront)
 9  X-Amz-Cf-Id: cz0twV2DdUinG-VzZD0bryhWIB8OcfoTBkPKbecD2TdkbvqWCvo7aw==
10  Connection: Keep-alive
11  {
12      "members":[
13          {
14              "accountId":"234567890123",
15              "detectorId":"12abc34d567e8fa901bc2d34e56789f0",
16              "email":"guarddutymember@amazon.com    ",
17              "relationshipStatus":"Monitored",
18              "invitedAt":"2018-02-09T21:33:05.568Z",
19              "masterId":"123456789012",
20              "updatedAt":"2018-02-09T21:33:46.363Z"
21          }
22      ],
23      "unprocessedAccounts":[
24
25      ]
26  }
```

GetThreatIntelSet

Returns the properties of the ThreatIntelSet that is specified by the ThreatIntelSet ID.

Important
If a user from a member account runs this API, the response contains the ThreatIntelSets uploaded by the master account. Currently in GuardDuty, users from member accounts CANNOT upload and further manage ThreatIntelSets. ThreatIntelSets that are uploaded by the master account are imposed on GuardDuty functionality in its member accounts. For more information, see Managing AWS Accounts in Amazon GuardDuty.

Request Syntax

```
1 GET https://<endpoint>/detector/{detectorId}/threatintelset/{threatIntelSetId}
```

Body:

```
1 detectorId : "string"
2 threatIntelSetId : "string"
```

Path Parameters

detectorId
The detector ID that specifies the GuardDuty service whose ThreatIntelSet properties you want to return.
Type: String
Required: Yes

threatIntelSetId
The unique ID that specifies the ThreatIntelSet whose properties you want to return.
Type: String
Required: Yes

Response Syntax

```
1 {
2     "name": "string",
3     "location": "string",
4     "format": "[TXT | STIX | OTX_CSV | ALIEN_VAULT | PROOF_POINT | FIRE_EYE]",
5     "status": "[INACTIVE | ACTIVATING | ACTIVE | DEACTIVATING | ERROR | DELETE_PENDING | DELETED
        ]"
6 }
```

Response Elements

If the action is successful, the service sends back an HTTP 200 response.

The following data is returned in JSON format by the service.

name
The name of the ThreatIntelSet.
Type: String

location
The URI of the file that contains the ThreatIntelSet.
Type: String

format

The format of the file that contains the ThreatIntelSet.

Type: String

Valid values: `TXT` | `STIX` | `OTX_CSV` | `ALIEN_VAULT` | `PROOF_POINT` | `FIRE_EYE`

status

The current status of the `ThreatIntelSet`.

Type: String

Valid values: `INACTIVE` | `ACTIVATING` | `ACTIVE` | `DEACTIVATING` | `ERROR` | `DELETE_PENDING` | `DELETED`

Errors

If the action is not successful, the service sends back an HTTP error response code along with detailed error information.

InvalidInputException

The request is rejected. An invalid or out-of-range value is specified as an input parameter.

HTTP Status Code: 400

InvalidInputException

The request is rejected. The required query or path parameters are not specified.

HTTP Status Code: 400

InvalidInputException

The request is rejected. One or more input parameters have invalid values.

HTTP Status Code: 400

InvalidInputException

The request is rejected. The parameter `detectorId` has an invalid value.

HTTP Status Code: 400

InvalidInputException

The request is rejected. An invalid `threatIntelSetId` is specified.

HTTP Status Code: 400

NoSuchEntityException

The request is rejected. The input `detectorId` is not owned by the current account.

HTTP Status Code: 400

NoSuchEntityException

The request is rejected. An invalid `threatIntelSetId` is specified.

HTTP Status Code: 400

InternalException

Internal server error.

HTTP Status Code: 500

Example

Sample Request

```
1 GET /detector/12abc34d567e8fa901bc2d34e56789f0/threatintelset/8cb094db7082fd0db09479755d215dba
      HTTP/1.1
2 Host: guardduty.us-west-2.amazonaws.com
3 Accept-Encoding: identity
4 Authorization: AUTHPARAMS
5 X-Amz-Date: 20180124T200105Z
6 User-Agent: aws-cli/1.14.29 Python/2.7.9 Windows/8 botocore/1.8.33
```

Sample Response

```
1  HTTP/1.1 200 OK
2  Content-Type: application/json
3  Content-Length: 137
4  Date: Wed, 24 Jan 2018 20:01:06 GMT
5  x-amzn-RequestId: 5040403c-0141-11e8-a09c-f1d8e1e0b9aa
6  X-Amzn-Trace-Id: sampled=0;root=1-5a68e602-a127df9b53e8b229624cd03e
7  X-Cache: Miss from cloudfront
8  Via: 1.1 08f323eee70ddda7af34d5feb414ce27.cloudfront.net (CloudFront)
9  X-Amz-Cf-Id: njPvvQsAq4ShiJcvOx0wF6WMmxdqrMHTnzX7Utni7r2_EFFVmsfn6w==
10 Connection: Keep-alive
11 {
12    "name":"ThreatIntelSet",
13    "location":"https://s3.amazonaws.com/guarddutylists/threatintelset.txt",
14    "format":"TXT",
15    "status":"ACTIVE"
16 }
```

InviteMembers

Invites other AWS accounts to enable Amazon GuardDuty and become GuardDuty member accounts. When an account accepts the invitation and becomes a member account, the master account can view and manage the GuardDuty findings of the member account.

Request Syntax

```
1 POST https://<endpoint>/detector/{detectorId}/member/invite
```

Body:

```
1 {
2     "accountIds": [
3         {
4             "accountId": "string"
5         },
6         "message": "string",
7         "disableEmailNotification": "boolean"
8     ]
9 }
```

Path Parameters

detectorID
The detector ID of the GuardDuty account that you want to use to invite members.
Required: Yes
Type: String

Request Parameters

The request accepts the following data in JSON format.

accountIds
A list of IDs of the AWS accounts that you want to invite to GuardDuty as members.
Type: Array of stings
Required: Yes
accountID
The AWS account ID.
Type: String

message
The invitation message that gets sent to the accounts that you want to invite to GuardDuty as members.
Type: String
Required: No

disableEmailNotification
Specifies whether an email notification is sent to the accounts that you want to invite to GuardDuty as members. When set to 'True', email notification is not sent to the invitees.
Type: Boolean
Required: No

Response Syntax

```
{
    "unprocessedAccounts": [
        {
            "accountId": "string",
            "result": "string"
        }
    ]
}
```

Response Elements

If the action is successful, the service sends back an HTTP 200 response.

The following data is returned in JSON format by the service.

unprocessedAccounts
A list of account ID and email address pairs of the AWS accounts that could not be processed.
Type: Array of strings
accountID
The ID of the AWS account that could not be processed.
Type: String
result
The reason why the AWS account could not be processed.
Type: String

Errors

If the action is not successful, the service sends back an HTTP error response code along with detailed error information.

InvalidInputException

The request is rejected. The current account cannot invite other accounts because it is already a member of another master account.

HTTP Status Code: 200

InvalidInputException

The request is rejected. The current account cannot invite itself.

HTTP Status Code: 200

InvalidInputException

The request is rejected. The member account's email address is missing.

HTTP Status Code: 200

InvalidInputException

The request is rejected. The current account has already invited or is already the GuardDuty master account of the specified member account ID.

HTTP Status Code: 200

InvalidInputException

The request is rejected. An invalid or out-of-range value is specified as an input parameter.

HTTP Status Code: 400

InvalidInputException

The request is rejected. The required query or path parameters are not specified.

HTTP Status Code: 400

InvalidInputException

The request is rejected. One or more input parameters have invalid values.

HTTP Status Code: 400

InvalidInputException

The request is rejected. The parameter `detectorId` has an invalid value.

HTTP Status Code: 400

NoSuchEntityException

The request is rejected. The input `detectorId` is not owned by the current account.

HTTP Status Code: 400

InternalException

Internal server error.

HTTP Status Code: 500

Example

Sample Request

```
1 POST /detector/12abc34d567e8fa901bc2d34e56789f0/member/invite HTTP/1.1
2 Host: guardduty.us-west-2.amazonaws.com
3 Accept-Encoding: identity
4 Content-Length: 32
5 Authorization: AUTHPARAMS
6 X-Amz-Date: 20180125T195805Z
7 User-Agent: aws-cli/1.14.29 Python/2.7.9 Windows/8 botocore/1.8.33
8 {
9     "accountIds":[
10        "123456789012"
11    ]
12 }
```

Sample Response

```
1 HTTP/1.1 200 OK
2 Content-Type: application/json
3 Content-Length: 26
4 Date: Thu, 25 Jan 2018 19:58:07 GMT
5 x-amzn-RequestId: 0f8d5826-020a-11e8-9b8e-6f87dff9eb0a
6 X-Amzn-Trace-Id: sampled=0;root=1-5a6a36ce-a5c2cd953fa214895696b609
7 X-Cache: Miss from cloudfront
8 Via: 1.1 202cd4e04661f12af0f4ce368b4e0a6d.cloudfront.net (CloudFront)
9 X-Amz-Cf-Id: JvaX4jhSDucSDIuL20JewNHkfTE7Gi_Xea14f9KncHhAO5pl7UkyVA==
10 Connection: Keep-alive
11 {
```

```
12    "unprocessedAccounts":[
13
14    ]
15 }
```

ListDetectors

Lists the detector IDs of enabled Amazon GuardDuty detectors in an AWS account.

Important
Currently, GuardDuty supports only one detector resource per AWS account per region.

Request Syntax

```
1 GET https://<endpoint>/detector
```

Body:

```
1 {
2     "maxResults": "integer",
3     "nextToken": "string"
4 }
```

Request Parameters

The request accepts the following data in JSON format.

maxResults
Indicates the maximum number of items that you want in the response.
Type: Integer
Required: No
Default: 50
Constraints: Minimum value is 1. Maximum value is 50.

nextToken
Paginates results. Set the value of this parameter to NULL on your first call to the `ListDetectors` operation. For subsequent calls to the operation, fill `nextToken` in the request with the value of `NextToken` from the previous response to continue listing data.
Type: String
Required: No

Response Syntax

Body:

```
1 {
2     "detectorIds": [list of detector IDs]
3 }
```

Response Elements

If the action is successful, the service sends back an HTTP 200 response.

The response is the following data in JSON format.

detectorIds
The list of all enabled detector IDs.
Type: Array of strings

nextToken

The token that is required for pagination.

Type: String

Errors

If the action is not successful, the service sends back an HTTP error response code along with detailed error information.

InvalidInputException

The request is rejected. An invalid or out-of-range value is specified as an input parameter.

HTTP Status Code: 400

InvalidInputException

The request is rejected. The required query or path parameters are not specified.

HTTP Status Code: 400

InvalidInputException

The request is rejected. One or more input parameters have invalid values.

HTTP Status Code: 400

InvalidInputException

The request is rejected. The parameter `maxResults` has an invalid value.

HTTP Status Code: 400

InvalidInputException

The request is rejected. The parameter `maxResults` is out-of-bounds.

HTTP Status Code: 400

InternalException

Internal server error.

HTTP Status Code: 500

Example

Sample Request

```
1 GET /detector HTTP/1.1
2 Host: guardduty.us-west-2.amazonaws.com
3 Accept-Encoding: identity
4 Authorization: AUTHPARAMS
5 X-Amz-Date: 20180123T230745Z
6 User-Agent: aws-cli/1.14.29 Python/2.7.9 Windows/8 botocore/1.8.33
```

Sample Response

```
1 HTTP/1.1 200 OK
2 Content-Type: application/json
3 Content-Length: 52
4 Date: Tue, 23 Jan 2018 23:07:46 GMT
5 x-amzn-RequestId: 397d0549-0092-11e8-a0ee-a7f9aa6e7572
```

```
 6 X-Amzn-Trace-Id: sampled=0;root=1-5a67c042-3405ff97a36fd78ee5cce278
 7 X-Cache: Miss from cloudfront
 8 Via: 1.1 bdf69c9338fccde2f01f587a28200671.cloudfront.net (CloudFront)
 9 X-Amz-Cf-Id: 4iF3SMkI1xcf_P7mLPyoj5cCpLdx--TiMJUrVKdNf3lpCdCVJCNLgQ==
10 Connection: Keep-alive
11 {
12     "detectorIds":[
13         "12abc34d567e8fa901bc2d34e56789f0"
14     ]
15 }
```

ListFilters

Returns a paginated list of the current filters.

Request Syntax

```
1 GET https://<endpoint>/detector/{detectorId}/filter?maxResults=&nextToken=
```

Body:

```
1 {
2     "filterNames": [
3         "string"
4     ],
5     "nextToken": "string"
6 }
```

Path Parameters

detectorId
The ID of the detector that specifies the GuardDuty service where you want to list filters.
Type: String
Required: Yes

maxResults
Indicates the maximum number of items that you want in the response.
Type: Integer
Required: No
Default: 50
Constraints: Minimum value is 1. Maximum value is 50.

nextToken
Paginates results. Set the value of this parameter to NULL on your first call to the **ListFilters** operation. For subsequent calls to the operation, fill **nextToken** in the request with the value of **nextToken** from the previous response to continue listing data.
Type: String
Required: No

Response Syntax

```
1 {
2     "filterNames": [
3         "string"
4     ],
5     "nextToken": "string"
6 }
```

Response Elements

If the action is successful, the service sends back an HTTP 200 response.

The following data is returned in JSON format by the service.

filterNames
A list of filter names.
Type: Array of strings

nextToken
The token that is required for pagination.
Type: String

Errors

If the action is not successful, the service sends back an HTTP error response code along with detailed error information.

InvalidInputException

The request is rejected. An invalid or out-of-range value is specified as an input parameter.

HTTP Status Code: 400

InvalidInputException

The request is rejected. The required query or path parameters are not specified.

HTTP Status Code: 400

InvalidInputException

The request is rejected. One or more input parameters have invalid values.

HTTP Status Code: 400

InvalidInputException

The request is rejected. The parameter `detectorId` has an invalid value.

HTTP Status Code: 400

InvalidInputException

The request is rejected. The parameter `maxResults` has an invalid value.

HTTP Status Code: 400

InvalidInputException

The request is rejected. The parameter `maxResults` is out-of-bounds.

HTTP Status Code: 400

InvalidInputException

The request is rejected. The parameter `nextToken` has an invalid value.

HTTP Status Code: 400

NoSuchEntityException

The request is rejected. The input `detectorId` is not owned by the current account.

HTTP Status Code: 400

InternalException

Internal server error.

HTTP Status Code: 500

ListFindings

Lists Amazon GuardDuty findings for the specified detector ID.

Request Syntax

```
1  POST https://<endpoint>/detector/{detectorId}/findings
```

Body:

```
1  {
2      "findingCriteria": {
3          "criterion": {
4              "<field>": {
5                  "Gt": "integer",
6                  "Gte": "integer",
7                  "Lt": "integer",
8                  "Lte": "integer",
9                  "Eq": [
10                     "string"
11                 ],
12                 "Neq": [
13                     "string"
14                 ]
15             }
16         }
17     },
18     "sortCriteria": {
19         "attributeName": "string",
20         "orderBy": "[ASC|DESC]"
21     },
22     "maxResults": "integer",
23     "nextToken": "string"
24 }
```

Path Parameters

detectorId
The ID of the detector that specifies the GuardDuty service whose findings you want to list.
Type: String
Required: Yes

Request Parameters

The request accepts the following data in JSON format.

maxResults
Indicates the maximum number of items that you want in the response.
Type: Integer
Required: No
Default: 50
Constraints: Minimum value is 1. Maximum value is 50.

nextToken

Paginates results. Set the value of this parameter to NULL on your first call to the `ListFindings` operation. For subsequent calls to the operation, fill `nextToken` in the request with the value of `nextToken` from the previous response to continue listing data.

Type: String

Required: No

findingCriteria

Represents the criteria used for querying findings.

Type: FindingCriteria

Required: No

You can only use the following attributes to query findings:

[See the AWS documentation website for more details]

Gt

Represents the "greater than" condition to be applied to a single field when querying for findings.

Required: No

Gte

Represents the "greater than equal" condition to be applied to a single field when querying for findings.

Required: No

Lt

Represents the "less than" condition to be applied to a single field when querying for findings.

Required: No

Lte

Represents the "less than equal" condition to be applied to a single field when querying for findings.

Required: No

Eq

Represents the "equal to" condition to be applied to a single field when querying for findings.

Required: No

Neq

Represents the "not equal to" condition to be applied to a single field when querying for findings.

Required: No

sortCriteria

Represents the criteria used for sorting findings.

Type: SortCriteria

Required: No

attributeName

Represents the parameter in a finding that can be queried.

Type: String

Required: No

orderBy

Represents the order of the sorting request.

Valid values: ASC | DESC

Type: String

Required: No

Response Syntax

```
1 {
2     "findingIds": [
3         "string"
4     ],
5     "nextToken": "string"
6 }
```

Response Elements

If the action is successful, the service sends back an HTTP 200 response.

The following data is returned in JSON format by the service.

findingIds
A list of IDs that specify the findings that are returned by the operation.
Type: Array of strings

nextToken
The token that is required for pagination.
Type: String

Errors

If the action is not successful, the service sends back an HTTP error response code along with detailed error information.

InvalidInputException

The request is rejected. An invalid or out-of-range value is specified as an input parameter.

HTTP Status Code: 400

InvalidInputException

The request is rejected. The required query or path parameters are not specified.

HTTP Status Code: 400

InvalidInputException

The request is rejected. One or more input parameters have invalid values.

HTTP Status Code: 400

InvalidInputException

The request is rejected. The parameter `detectorId` has an invalid value.

HTTP Status Code: 400

InvalidInputException

The request is rejected. The parameter `maxResults` has an invalid value.

HTTP Status Code: 400

InvalidInputException

The request is rejected. The parameter `maxResults` is out-of-bounds.

HTTP Status Code: 400

InvalidInputException

The request is rejected. The parameter `findingCriteria` has an invalid value.

HTTP Status Code: 400

InvalidInputException

The request is rejected. The parameter `sortCriteria` has an invalid value.

HTTP Status Code: 400

NoSuchEntityException

The request is rejected. The input `detectorId` is not owned by the current account.

HTTP Status Code: 400

InternalException

Internal server error.

HTTP Status Code: 500

Example

Sample Request

```
1 POST /detector/12abc34d567e8fa901bc2d34e56789f0/findings HTTP/1.1
2 Host: guardduty.us-west-2.amazonaws.com
3 Accept-Encoding: identity
4 Content-Length: 70
5 Authorization: AUTHPARAMS
6 X-Amz-Date: 20180212T223938Z
7 User-Agent: aws-cli/1.14.29 Python/2.7.9 Windows/8 botocore/1.8.33
8 {
9     "findingCriteria":{
10        "criterion":{
11           "updatedAt":{
12              "gte":1486685375
13           }
14        }
15     }
16 }
```

Sample Response

```
1 HTTP/1.1 200 OK
2 Content-Type: application/json
3 Content-Length: 1746
4 Date: Mon, 12 Feb 2018 22:39:39 GMT
5 x-amzn-RequestId: 9c063378-1045-11e8-912b-55dcb9d58ea1
6 X-Amzn-Trace-Id: sampled=0;root=1-5a8217ab-91c20067a9d784bf259099f2
7 X-Cache: Miss from cloudfront
8 Via: 1.1 1a1272478361d8461b68eec8a4e3b072.cloudfront.net (CloudFront)
9 X-Amz-Cf-Id: hJB2P8k3QOSuLXimNeOn2EuBvz_ixcnsaOHW1pBZ7KNnPYPdTEOrEA==
10 Connection: Keep-alive
11 {
12    "findingIds":[
13       "d4b0be682aeeb94e06ff046f3b720aaf",
14       "40b0be6cfea750c084aae20c21ace107",
15       "cab0be7a06e5ebe1d8911cadbfbd51c8",
16       "d0b0c39ae57fb67f9edbd2622961771d",
17       "14b0be677c07323d61d7006cce074238",
18       "6eb0be66d03c7b27037f8609875c9bf7",
19       "c4b0be6e6177dd4e269da24de95c933e",
20       "64b0c3bb2da01d83eb306d067ea73e67",
21       "3ab0c0e7734ccbda8f7074952063a45f",
22       "38b0c0ce04f29861dc6331631a233b6b",
23       "4cb0c28afacdfc4bb5577b224e0e52ae",
24       "94b0c2305c7d6ff1e3d483e7f36a5238",
```

```
25        "72b0c1f80a23ca9082133c46c7558666",
26        "d6b0c1910d5faeb6e89fe40bd78a35e6",
27        "14b0c18efa4f2981d44b2131a560b73a",
28        "9cb0be64df8ba1df249c45eb8a0bf584",
29        "08b0be64df8b46440d718fc5e33e449c",
30        "70b0be64df8b3342472e966717a5f2d8",
31        "86b0be64df8ae19c13c4d55080b48e6a",
32        "e6b0be64df8ae6744746c151aebbef4c",
33        "36b0be64df8a1f72cbc32e723c2d8b89",
34        "4cb0be64df8a20484f3a1f7ad816ca96",
35        "5cb0be64df8a6b5c3da491b5599fc8ae",
36        "44b0be64df89360da7c31819b3f515fa",
37        "76b0be64df89cc6ffa31a5d34888368c",
38        "0eb0be64df890a043aef0b1b807ddfc7",
39        "ceb0be64df894fdef2500c7ffcc44b84",
40        "32b0be64df88b6c6e8bbc29a798739ca",
41        "50b0be64df88991e0221f80f4288441d",
42        "72b0be64df88753b1aa9146729bc2fcc",
43        "fab0be64df887026d806b6553d67bacb",
44        "2ab0be64df878810cbe619a0ba7ef05d",
45        "78b0be64df87ab9eb027d0c0820433d6",
46        "3eb0be64df872fa74d318e6e31d03728",
47        "40b0be64df8746cdecf990d3f89fe633",
48        "56b0be64df86ad5f22e15c17b381bd8c",
49        "9eb0be64df8693f01ade916097512133",
50        "d2b0be64df86145bbafa2f2ea9e05dba",
51        "d8b0be64df85da2fb107ee60013fef4d",
52        "f0b0be64df864f7d6c70d0adc21ec430",
53        "aeb0be64df85d6365eb815b1bef28dff",
54        "ccb0be64df85e42caf8e33b916eaf7d1",
55        "2cb0be64df852627bbb68f63749b36e0",
56        "90b0be64df8513c19d6864ea3a02b91f",
57        "7ab0be64df84dd2cb89e38547264e956",
58        "94b0be64df84c4e7ce9f49f95b58b4ac",
59        "92b0be64df846c83bd36dca0d7cd8271",
60        "ccb0be64df845a4ed9258957024d0a5b",
61        "50b0be64df83e63bb9693bb63b2e9faa"
62    ],
63    "nextToken":""
64 }
```

ListInvitations

Lists all Amazon GuardDuty membership invitations that were sent to the current AWS account.

Request Syntax

```
1 GET https://<endpoint>/invitation
```

Body:

```
1 {
2     "maxResults" : "integer",
3     "nextToken" : "string"
4 }
```

Request Parameters

The request accepts the following data in JSON format.

maxResults
Indicates the maximum number of items that you want in the response.
Type: Integer
Required: No
Default: 50
Constraints: Minimum value is 1. Maximum value is 50.

nextToken
Paginates results. Set the value of this parameter to NULL on your first call to the `ListInvitations` operation. For subsequent calls to the operation, fill `nextToken` in the request with the value of `NextToken` from the previous response to continue listing data.
Required: No
Type: String

Response Syntax

```
1 {
2     "invitations": [
3         {
4             "accountId": "string",
5             "invitationId": "string",
6             "invitedAt": "string",
7             "relationshipStatus": "string"
8         }
9     ],
10     "nextToken": "string"
11 }
```

Response Elements

If the action is successful, the service sends back an HTTP 200 response.

The following data is returned in JSON format by the service.

invitations

A list of details about GuardDuty membership invitations that were sent to this AWS account.

Type: Array

accountId

The ID of the AWS account that sent the invitation.

Type: String

invitationId

The unique ID of the invitation.

Type: String

invitedAt

The time stamp at which the invitation was sent.

Type: String

relationshipStatus

The current relationship status between the inviter and invitee accounts. Valid values: `CREATED` | `INVITED` | `DISABLED` | `ENABLED` | `REMOVED` | `RESIGNED` | `EMAILVERIFICATIONINPROGRESS` | `EMAILVERIFICATIONFAILED`

Type: String

nextToken

When a response is generated, if there is more data to be listed, this parameter is present in the response and contains the value to use for the `nextToken` parameter in a subsequent pagination request. If there is no more data to be listed, this parameter is set to NULL.

Type: String

Errors

If the action is not successful, the service sends back an HTTP error response code along with detailed error information.

InvalidInputException

The request is rejected. An invalid or out-of-range value is specified as an input parameter.

HTTP Status Code: 400

InvalidInputException

The request is rejected. The required query or path parameters are not specified.

HTTP Status Code: 400

InvalidInputException

The request is rejected. One or more input parameters have invalid values.

HTTP Status Code: 400

InvalidInputException

The request is rejected. The parameter `maxResults` has an invalid value.

HTTP Status Code: 400

InvalidInputException

The request is rejected. The parameter `maxResults` is out-of-bounds.

HTTP Status Code: 400

InternalException

Internal server error.

HTTP Status Code: 500

Example

Sample Request

```
1 GET /invitation HTTP/1.1
2 Host: guardduty.us-west-2.amazonaws.com
3 Accept-Encoding: identity
4 Authorization: AUTHPARAMS
5 X-Amz-Date: 20180125T201238Z
6 User-Agent: aws-cli/1.14.29 Python/2.7.9 Windows/8 botocore/1.8.33
```

Sample Response

```
1  HTTP/1.1 200 OK
2  Content-Type: application/json
3  Content-Length: 180
4  Date: Thu, 25 Jan 2018 20:12:39 GMT
5  x-amzn-RequestId: 176ef1d7-020c-11e8-8ed9-eb03a370f9db
6  X-Amzn-Trace-Id: sampled=0;root=1-5a6a3a37-ce08a19c90097c2711af6d20
7  X-Cache: Miss from cloudfront
8  Via: 1.1 8a4a49fefe26d51023ff83ac514d5779.cloudfront.net (CloudFront)
9  X-Amz-Cf-Id: 6lDytN8vgXTKCeKmTKW6n9uu-Q8auCCDJENKQ46nagklpnjkeIuFkA==
10 Connection: Keep-alive
11 {
12    "invitations":[
13      {
14         "accountId":"6012345678901",
15         "invitationId":"2cb097774d0b74808af8fa270f1dc404",
16         "invitedAt":"2018-01-25T20:07:24.438Z",
17         "relationshipStatus":"Invited"
18      }
19    ],
20    "empty":false
21 }
```

ListIPSets

Lists the IPSet of the Amazon GuardDuty service that is specified by the detector ID.

Important
If a user from a member account runs this API, the response contains the IPSets uploaded by the master account. Currently in GuardDuty, users from member accounts CANNOT upload and further manage IPSets. IPSets that are uploaded by the master account are imposed on GuardDuty functionality in its member accounts. For more information, see Managing AWS Accounts in Amazon GuardDuty.

Request Syntax

Path parameters:

```
1 GET https://<endpoint>/detector/{detectorId}/ipset
```

Body:

```
1 {
2     "maxResults": "integer",
3     "nextToken": "string"
4 }
```

Path Parameters

detectorId
The detector ID that specifies the GuardDuty service whose IPSet objects you want to list.
Type: String
Required: Yes

Request Parameters

The request accepts the following data in JSON format.

maxResults
Indicates the maximum number of items that you want in the response.
Type: Integer
Required: No
Default: 50
Constraints: Minimum value is 1. Maximum value is 50.

nextToken
Paginates results. Set the value of this parameter to NULL on your first call to the `ListIPSets` operation. For subsequent calls to the operation, fill `nextToken` in the request with the value of `NextToken` from the previous response to continue listing data.
Type: String
Required: No

Response Syntax

```
1 {
2     "ipSetIds": [
3         "string"
4     ],
5     "nextToken": "string"
6 }
```

Response Elements

If the action is successful, the service sends back an HTTP 200 response.

The following data is returned in JSON format by the service.

ipSetIds
A list of IDs that specify the IPSet objects of the specified GuardDuty service.
Type: Array of strings

nextToken
The token that is required for pagination.
Type: String

Errors

If the action is not successful, the service sends back an HTTP error response code along with detailed error information.

InvalidInputException

The request is rejected. An invalid or out-of-range value is specified as an input parameter.

HTTP Status Code: 400

InvalidInputException

The request is rejected. The required query or path parameters are not specified.

HTTP Status Code: 400

InvalidInputException

The request is rejected. One or more input parameters have invalid values.

HTTP Status Code: 400

InvalidInputException

The request is rejected. The parameter `detectorId` has an invalid value.

HTTP Status Code: 400

InvalidInputException

The request is rejected. The parameter `maxResults` has an invalid value.

HTTP Status Code: 400

InvalidInputException

The request is rejected. The parameter `maxResults` is out-of-bounds.

HTTP Status Code: 400

NoSuchEntityException

The request is rejected. The input `detectorId` is not owned by the current account.

HTTP Status Code: 400

InternalException

Internal server error.

HTTP Status Code: 500

Example

Sample Request

```
1 GET /detector/26b092acdf3e60c625b69013f7488f7b/ipset HTTP/1.1
2 Host: guardduty.us-west-2.amazonaws.com
3 Accept-Encoding: identity
4 Authorization: AUTHPARAMS
5 X-Amz-Date: 20180124T001914Z
6 User-Agent: aws-cli/1.14.29 Python/2.7.9 Windows/8 botocore/1.8.33
```

Sample Response

```
1 HTTP/1.1 200 OK
2 Content-Type: application/json
3 Content-Length: 66
4 Date: Wed, 24 Jan 2018 00:19:16 GMT
5 x-amzn-RequestId: 3655f06a-009c-11e8-b1c0-63f7fc930fe2
6 X-Amzn-Trace-Id: sampled=0;root=1-5a67d104-81ea75e98e2fe32d09842944
7 X-Cache: Miss from cloudfront
8 Via: 1.1 5b51f6e8f38342d63beb93a0db7a392b.cloudfront.net (CloudFront)
9 X-Amz-Cf-Id: RPe-C-TRFt4cMylGV8ux1PCoeG5eK1seeolplZTVhYTtRZLEkDUd6w==
10 Connection: Keep-alive
11 {
12   "ipSetId":"0cb0141ab9fbde177613ab9436212e90"
13 }
```

ListMembers

Lists details about all member accounts for the current Amazon GuardDuty master account.

Request Syntax

```
1 GET https://<endpoint>/detector/{detectorId}/member
```

Body:

```
1 {
2     "maxResults": "integer",
3     "nextToken": "string",
4     "onlyAssociated": "boolean"
5 }
```

Path Parameters

detectorID
The detector ID of the GuardDuty account whose members you want to list.
Required: Yes
Type: String

Request Parameters

The request accepts the following data in JSON format.

maxResults
Indicates the maximum number of items that you want in the response.
Required: No
Type: String
Default: 50
Constraints: Minimum value is 1. Maximum value is 50.

nextToken
Paginates results. Set the value of this parameter to NULL on your first call to the `ListMembers` operation. For subsequent calls to the operation, fill `nextToken` in the request with the value of `NextToken` from the previous response to continue listing data.
Required: No
Type: String

onlyAssociated
Specifies what member accounts the response includes based on their relationship status with the master account. The default value is TRUE. If `onlyAssociated` is set to TRUE, the response includes member accounts whose relationship status with the master is set to `ENABLED` or `DISABLED`. If `onlyAssociated` is set to FALSE, the response includes all existing member accounts.
Required: No
Type: Boolean
Default: True

Response Syntax

```
1  {
2      "members": [
3          {
4              "accountId": "string",
5              "detectorId": "string",
6              "email": "string",
7              "masterId": "string",
8              "relationshipStatus": "string",
9              "invitedAt": "string",
10             "updatedAt": "string"
11         }
12     ],
13     "nextToken": "string"
14 }
```

Response Elements

If the action is successful, the service sends back an HTTP 200 response.

The following data is returned in JSON format by the service.

members
A list of details about the GuardDuty member accounts.
Type: Array
accountId
The AWS account ID.
Type: String
detectorId
The unique ID of the GuardDuty member account.
Type: String
email
The email address of the GuardDuty member account.
Type: String
masterId
The account ID of the master GuardDuty for a member account.
Type: String
relationshipStatus
The status of the relationship between the member account and its master account. Valid values:
`CREATED` | `INVITED` | `DISABLED` | `ENABLED` | `REMOVED` | `RESIGNED` | `EMAILVERIFICATIONINPROGRESS` |
`EMAILVERIFICATIONFAILED`
Type: String
invitedAt
Time stamp at which the member account was invited to GuardDuty.
Type: ISO 8601 string format: YYYY-MM-DDTHH:MM:SS.SSSZ or YYYY-MM-DDTHH:MM:SSZ depending on whether the value contains milliseconds.
updatedAt
Time stamp at which this member account was updated.
Type: ISO 8601 string format: YYYY-MM-DDTHH:MM:SS.SSSZ or YYYY-MM-DDTHH:MM:SSZ depending on whether the value contains milliseconds.

nextToken
The token that is required for pagination. When a response is generated, if there is more data to be listed, this parameter is present in the response and contains the value to use for the `nextToken` parameter in a subsequent pagination request. If there is no more data to be listed, this parameter is set to NULL.
Type: Integer

Errors

If the action is not successful, the service sends back an HTTP error response code along with detailed error information.

InvalidInputException

The request is rejected. An invalid or out-of-range value is specified as an input parameter.

HTTP Status Code: 400

InvalidInputException

The request is rejected. The required query or path parameters are not specified.

HTTP Status Code: 400

InvalidInputException

The request is rejected. One or more input parameters have invalid values.

HTTP Status Code: 400

InvalidInputException

The request is rejected. The parameter `detectorId` has an invalid value.

HTTP Status Code: 400

InvalidInputException

The request is rejected. The parameter `maxResults` has an invalid value.

HTTP Status Code: 400

InvalidInputException

The request is rejected. The parameter `maxResults` is out-of-bounds.

HTTP Status Code: 400

InvalidInputException

The request is rejected. The parameter `onlyAssociated` has an invalid value.

HTTP Status Code: 400

NoSuchEntryException

The request is rejected. The input `detectorId` is not owned by the current account.

HTTP Status Code: 400

InternalException

Internal server error.

HTTP Status Code: 500

Example

Sample Request

```
1 GET /detector/26b092acdf3e60c625b69013f7488f7b/member HTTP/1.1
2 Host: guardduty.us-west-2.amazonaws.com
3 Accept-Encoding: identity
4 Authorization: AUTHPARAMS
5 X-Amz-Date: 20180209T214335Z
```

6 User-Agent: aws-cli/1.14.29 Python/2.7.9 Windows/8 botocore/1.8.33

Sample Response

```
 1 HTTP/1.1 200 OK
 2 Content-Type: application/json
 3 Content-Length: 256
 4 Date: Fri, 09 Feb 2018 21:43:37 GMT
 5 x-amzn-RequestId: 48c4d871-0de2-11e8-a0da-35504ea5b4f3
 6 X-Amzn-Trace-Id: sampled=0;root=1-5a7e1608-de91dbb494298683e2ba0b97
 7 X-Cache: Miss from cloudfront
 8 Via: 1.1 a8a06e035420932f2808c2efee52f455.cloudfront.net (CloudFront)
 9 X-Amz-Cf-Id: _tzbuMnoMN2zwkakGIqpbLEODd2sbIyiJ3dj2c3anx_Db7MNmrlNCQ==
10 Connection: Keep-alive
11 {
12    "members":[
13       {
14          "accountId":"123456789012",
15          "detectorId":"12abc34d567e8fa901bc2d34e56789f0",
16          "email":"guarddutymember@amazon.com",
17          "relationshipStatus":"Enabled",
18          "invitedAt":"2018-02-09T21:33:05.568Z",
19          "masterId":"234567890123",
20          "updatedAt":"2018-02-09T21:33:46.363Z"
21       }
22    ]
23 }
```

ListThreatIntelSets

Lists the ThreatIntelSets of the GuardDuty service that are specified by the detector ID.

Important

If a user from a member account runs this API, the response contains the ThreatIntelSets uploaded by the master account. Currently in GuardDuty, users from member accounts CANNOT upload and further manage ThreatIntelSets. ThreatIntelSets that are uploaded by the master account are imposed on GuardDuty functionality in its member accounts. For more information, see Managing AWS Accounts in Amazon GuardDuty.

Request Syntax

```
1 GET https://<endpoint>/detector/{detectorId}/threatintelset
```

Body:

```
1 {
2     "maxResults": "integer",
3     "nextToken": "string"
4 }
```

Path Parameters

detectorId
The detector ID that specifies the GuardDuty service whose ThreatIntelSets you want to list.
Type: String
Required: Yes

Request Parameters

The request accepts the following data in JSON format.

maxResults
Indicates the maximum number of items that you want in the response.
Type: Integer
Required: No
Default: 50
Constraints: Minimum value is 1. Maximum value is 50.

nextToken
Paginates results. Set the value of this parameter to NULL on your first call to the `ListThreatIntelSets` operation. For subsequent calls to the action, fill `nextToken` in the request with the value of `NextToken` from the previous response to continue listing data.
Type: String
Required: No

Response Syntax

If the action is successful, the service sends back an HTTP 200 response.

```
1 {
2     "threatIntelSetIds": [
3         "string"
4     ],
```

```
5     "nextToken": "string"
6 }
```

Response Elements

The following data is returned in JSON format by the service.

threatIntelSetIds
A list of IDs that specify the ThreatIntelSet objects of the specified GuardDuty service.
Type: array of Strings
Constraints: Minimum number of 0 items. Maximum number of 50 items.

nextToken
The token that is required for pagination.
Type: String

Errors

If the action is not successful, the service sends back an HTTP error response code along with detailed error information.

InvalidInputException

The request is rejected. An invalid or out-of-range value is specified as an input parameter.

HTTP Status Code: 400

InvalidInputException

The request is rejected. The required query or path parameters are not specified.

HTTP Status Code: 400

InvalidInputException

The request is rejected. One or more input parameters have invalid values.

HTTP Status Code: 400

InvalidInputException

The request is rejected. The parameter `detectorId` has an invalid value.

HTTP Status Code: 400

InvalidInputException

The request is rejected. The parameter `maxResults` has an invalid value.

HTTP Status Code: 400

InvalidInputException

The request is rejected. The parameter `maxResults` is out-of-bounds.

HTTP Status Code: 400

NoSuchEntityException

The request is rejected. The input `detectorId` is not owned by the current account.

HTTP Status Code: 400

InternalException

Internal server error.

HTTP Status Code: 500

Example

Sample Request

```
1 GET /detector/12abc34d567e8fa901bc2d34e56789f0/threatintelset HTTP/1.1
2 Host: guardduty.us-west-2.amazonaws.com
3 Accept-Encoding: identity
4 Authorization: AUTHPARAMS
5 X-Amz-Date: 20180124T195513Z
6 User-Agent: aws-cli/1.14.29 Python/2.7.9 Windows/8 botocore/1.8.33
```

Sample Response

```
1  HTTP/1.1 200 OK
2  Content-Type: application/json
3  Content-Length: 75
4  Date: Wed, 24 Jan 2018 19:55:14 GMT
5  x-amzn-RequestId: 7e5a935c-0140-11e8-a9ab-51b1993e9c62
6  X-Amzn-Trace-Id: sampled=0;root=1-5a68e4a2-f59a246addd680e790b6c2e0
7  X-Cache: Miss from cloudfront
8  Via: 1.1 7cbd9c5a78702cfae1a7ed58e294736e.cloudfront.net (CloudFront)
9  X-Amz-Cf-Id: -LPBYOXNCOhOifRWzhb9Lo4HLRJA2BxaFfLzzvVeAhXrPkuqlcnBpg==
10 Connection: Keep-alive
11 {
12    "threatIntelSetIds":[
13       "8cb094db7082fd0db09479755d215dba"
14    ],
15    "nextToken":null
16 }
```

StartMonitoringMembers

Re-enables Amazon GuardDuty to monitor findings of the member accounts that are specified by the account IDs. A master GuardDuty account can run this command after disabling GuardDuty from monitoring the findings of these member accounts by running StopMonitoringMembers.

Request Syntax

```
POST https://<endpoint>/detector/{detectorId}/member/start
```

Body:

```
{
    "accountIds": [
        {
            "accountId": "string"
        }
    ]
}
```

Path Parameters

detectorID
The detector ID of the GuardDuty account that you want to stop from monitoring the findings of member accounts.
Type: String
Required: Yes

Request Parameters

The request accepts the following data in JSON format.

accountIds
A list of account IDs of the GuardDuty member accounts whose findings you want the master account to re-enable for monitoring.
Type: Array of strings
Required: Yes
accountID
The AWS account ID.
Type: String

Response Syntax

```
{
    "unprocessedAccounts": [
        {
            "accountId": "string",
            "result": "string"
        }
    ]
}
```

Response Elements

If the action is successful, the service sends back an HTTP 200 response.

The following data is returned in JSON format by the service.

unprocessedAccounts
A list of account ID and email address pairs of the AWS accounts that could not be processed.
Type: Array of strings
accountID
The ID of the AWS account that could not be processed.
Type: String
result
The reason why the AWS account could not be processed.
Type: String

Errors

If the action is not successful, the service sends back an HTTP error response code along with detailed error information.

InvalidInputException

The request is rejected. The specified account ID is not an associated member of the current account.

HTTP Status Code: 200

InvalidInputException

The request is rejected. The specified handshake role of the specified member account ID cannot be assumed by GuardDuty on behalf of the specified master account ID.

HTTP Status Code: 200

InvalidInputException

The request is rejected. An invalid or out-of-range value is specified as an input parameter.

HTTP Status Code: 400

InvalidInputException

The request is rejected. The required query or path parameters are not specified.

HTTP Status Code: 400

InvalidInputException

The request is rejected. One or more input parameters have invalid values.

HTTP Status Code: 400

InvalidInputException

The request is rejected. The parameter `detectorId` has an invalid value.

HTTP Status Code: 400

NoSuchEntityException

The request is rejected. The input `detectorId` is not owned by the current account.

HTTP Status Code: 400

InternalException

Internal server error.

HTTP Status Code: 500

Example

Sample Request

```
1 POST /detector/26b092acdf3e60c625b69013f7488f7b/member/start HTTP/1.1
2 Host: guardduty.us-west-2.amazonaws.com
3 Accept-Encoding: identity
4 Content-Length: 32
5 Authorization: AUTHPARAMS
6 X-Amz-Date: 20180209T215455Z
7 User-Agent: aws-cli/1.14.29 Python/2.7.9 Windows/8 botocore/1.8.33
8 {
9    "accountIds":[
10       "123456789012"
11    ]
12 }
```

Sample Response

```
1 HTTP/1.1 200 OK
2 Content-Type: application/json
3 Content-Length: 26
4 Date: Fri, 09 Feb 2018 21:54:56 GMT
5 x-amzn-RequestId: dde3efad-0de3-11e8-9ba1-c17118e93549
6 X-Amzn-Trace-Id: sampled=0;root=1-5a7e18b0-786dcf902e5059ee64f7e30a
7 X-Cache: Miss from cloudfront
8 Via: 1.1 b2532cb29a55e8fe8106a4a9a9241592.cloudfront.net (CloudFront)
9 X-Amz-Cf-Id: pSrlCyqEfDP1FOdZMXIafXMzF5nPf2DZrIatSiD4E5b9ZXFHd1Ot0w==
10 Connection: Keep-alive
11 {
12    "unprocessedAccounts":[
13
14    ]
15 }
```

StopMonitoringMembers

Disables Amazon GuardDuty from monitoring findings of the member accounts that are specified by the account IDs. After running this command, a master GuardDuty account can run StartMonitoringMembers to re-enable GuardDuty to monitor the findings of these members.

Request Syntax

```
1 POST https://<endpoint>/detector/{detectorId}/member/stop
```

Body:

```
1 {
2     "accountIds": [
3         {
4             "accountId": "string"
5         }
6     ]
7 }
```

Path Parameters

detectorID
The detector ID of the GuardDuty account that you want to stop from monitoring the findings of member accounts.
Type: String
Required: Yes

Request Parameters

The request accepts the following data in JSON format.

accountIds
A list of account IDs of the GuardDuty member accounts whose findings you want the master account to stop monitoring.
Type: Array of strings
Required: Yes
accountID
AWS account ID.
Type: String

Response Syntax

```
1 {
2     "unprocessedAccounts": [
3         {
4             "accountId": "string",
5             "result": "string"
6         }
7     ]
8 }
```

Response Elements

If the action is successful, the service sends back an HTTP 200 response.

The following data is returned in JSON format by the service.

unprocessedAccounts
A list of account ID and email address pairs of the AWS accounts that could not be processed.
Type: Array of strings
accountID
The ID of the AWS account that could not be processed.
Type: String
result
The reason why the AWS account could not be processed.
Type: String

Errors

If the action is not successful, the service sends back an HTTP error response code along with detailed error information.

InvalidInputException

The request is rejected. The specified account ID is not a member of the current account.

HTTP Status Code: 200

InvalidInputException

The request is rejected. The specified handshake role of the specified member account ID cannot be assumed by GuardDuty on behalf of the specified master account ID.

HTTP Status Code: 200

InvalidInputException

The request is rejected. An invalid or out-of-range value is specified as an input parameter.

HTTP Status Code: 400

InvalidInputException

The request is rejected. The required query or path parameters are not specified.

HTTP Status Code: 400

InvalidInputException

The request is rejected. One or more input parameters have invalid values.

HTTP Status Code: 400

InvalidInputException

The request is rejected. The parameter `detectorId` has an invalid value.

HTTP Status Code: 400

NoSuchEntityException

The request is rejected. The input `detectorId` is not owned by the current account.

HTTP Status Code: 400

InternalException

Internal server error.

HTTP Status Code: 500

Example

Sample Request

```
1 POST /detector/26b092acdf3e60c625b69013f7488f7b/member/stop HTTP/1.1
2 Host: guardduty.us-west-2.amazonaws.com
3 Accept-Encoding: identity
4 Content-Length: 32
5 Authorization: AUTHPARAMS
6 X-Amz-Date: 20180209T215008Z
7 User-Agent: aws-cli/1.14.29 Python/2.7.9 Windows/8 botocore/1.8.33
8 {
9    "accountIds":[
10       "123456789012"
11    ]
12 }
```

Sample Response

```
1 HTTP/1.1 200 OK
2 Content-Type: application/json
3 Content-Length: 26
4 Date: Fri, 09 Feb 2018 21:50:09 GMT
5 x-amzn-RequestId: 32b833a1-0de3-11e8-b5b7-6ffb530727e9
6 X-Amzn-Trace-Id: sampled=0;root=1-5a7e1791-5affbdd584be95ecf97cc9f2
7 X-Cache: Miss from cloudfront
8 Via: 1.1 4b41f5d4002cf5daabe6e170bd619abc.cloudfront.net (CloudFront)
9 X-Amz-Cf-Id: KhOTiBOnEjFXmBjANQOjIiYCE2fGOGiaFAKfetjK65Dv16VWeH4ESw==
10 Connection: Keep-alive
11 {
12    "unprocessedAccounts":[
13
14    ]
15 }
```

UnarchiveFindings

Unarchives Amazon GuardDuty findings that are specified by the list of finding IDs.

Request Syntax

Path parameters:

```
1 POST https://<endpoint>/detector/{detectorId}/findings/unarchive
```

Body:

```
1 {
2     "findingIds": [
3         "string"
4     ]
5 }
```

Path Parameters

detectorId
The ID of the detector that specifies the GuardDuty service whose findings you want to unarchive.
Required: Yes

Request Parameters

The request accepts the following data in JSON format.

findingIds
The IDs of the findings that you want to unarchive.
Type: Array of strings. Minimum number of 0 items. Maximum number of 50 items.
Required: Yes

Response Elements

If the action is successful, the service sends back an HTTP 200 response.

Errors

If the action is not successful, the service sends back an HTTP error response code along with detailed error information.

InvalidInputException

The request is rejected. An invalid or out-of-range value is specified as an input parameter.

HTTP Status Code: 400

InvalidInputException

The request is rejected. The required query or path parameters are not specified.

HTTP Status Code: 400

InvalidInputException

The request is rejected. One or more input parameters have invalid values.

HTTP Status Code: 400

InvalidInputException

The request is rejected. The parameter `detectorId` has an invalid value.

HTTP Status Code: 400

InvalidInputException

The request is rejected. The number of requested finding IDs is out-of-bounds.

HTTP Status Code: 400

NoSuchEntityException

The request is rejected. The input `detectorId` is not owned by the current account.

HTTP Status Code: 400

AccessDeniedException

The request is rejected. The caller is not authorized to call this API.

HTTP Status Code: 400

InternalException

Internal server error.

HTTP Status Code: 500

Example

Sample Request

```
1 POST /detector/c6b0be64463ff852400d8ae5b2353866/findings/unarchive HTTP/1.1
2 Host: guardduty.us-west-2.amazonaws.com
3 Accept-Encoding: identity
4 Content-Length: 52
5 Authorization: AUTHPARAMS
6 X-Amz-Date: 20180209T231331Z
7 User-Agent: aws-cli/1.14.29 Python/2.7.9 Windows/8 botocore/1.8.33
8 {
9   "findingIds":[
10     "9cb0be64df8ba1df249c45eb8a0bf584"
11   ]
12 }
```

Sample Response

```
1 HTTP/1.1 200 OK
2 Content-Type: application/json
3 Content-Length: 0
4 Date: Fri, 09 Feb 2018 23:13:32 GMT
5 x-amzn-RequestId: d8d7831e-0dee-11e8-b703-ab81f2419585
6 X-Amzn-Trace-Id: sampled=0;root=1-5a7e2b1c-5d5292523c568f02a266c57b
7 X-Cache: Miss from cloudfront
8 Via: 1.1 8a4a49fefe26d51023ff83ac514d5779.cloudfront.net (CloudFront)
```

```
 9 X-Amz-Cf-Id: WWIYv0gEFz8k9cuPE_FT54T1aDL80Nrpfn3bDVLW7s1AbuQzWcMhkg==
10 Connection: Keep-alive
```

UpdateDetector

Updates the Amazon GuardDuty detector that is specified by the detector ID.

Request Syntax

```
1 POST https://<endpoint>/detector/{detectorId}
```

Body:

```
1 {
2     "enable" : "boolean"
3 }
```

Path Parameters

detectorID
The unique ID of the detector that you want to update.
Type: String
Required: Yes

Request Parameters

The request accepts the following data in JSON format.

enable
Specifies whether the detector is enabled.
Type: Boolean
Required: No

Response Elements

If the action is successful, the service sends back an HTTP 200 response.

Errors

If the action is not successful, the service sends back an HTTP error response code along with detailed error information.

InvalidInputException

The request is rejected. An invalid or out-of-range value is specified as an input parameter.

HTTP Status Code: 400

InvalidInputException

The request is rejected. The required query or path parameters are not specified.

HTTP Status Code: 400

InvalidInputException

The request is rejected. One or more input parameters have invalid values.

HTTP Status Code: 400

InvalidInputException

The request is rejected. The parameter `detectorId` has an invalid value.

HTTP Status Code: 400

AccessDeniedException

The request is rejected. You do not have the required `iam:CreateServiceLinkedRole` permission.

HTTP Status Code: 400

NoSuchEntityException

The request is rejected. The input `detectorId` is not owned by the current account.

HTTP Status Code: 400

InternalException

Internal server error.

HTTP Status Code: 500

Example

Sample Request

```
1 POST /detector/12abc34d567e8fa901bc2d34e56789f0 HTTP/1.1
2 Host: guardduty.us-west-2.amazonaws.com
3 Accept-Encoding: identity
4 Content-Length: 16
5 Authorization: AUTHPARAMS
6 X-Amz-Date: 20180123T231356Z
7 User-Agent: aws-cli/1.14.29 Python/2.7.9 Windows/8 botocore/1.8.33
8 {
9     "enable":true
10 }
```

Sample Response

```
1 HTTP/1.1 200 OK
2 Content-Type: application/json
3 Content-Length: 0
4 Date: Tue, 23 Jan 2018 23:13:57 GMT
5 x-amzn-RequestId: 16c23992-0093-11e8-a33d-67e86e7cc0b9
6 X-Amzn-Trace-Id: sampled=0;root=1-5a67c1b5-f8ce3625e119d47f2531e4ac
7 X-Cache: Miss from cloudfront
8 Via: 1.1 b7b35e3be0ac217c56fb0eb4da9b75bb.cloudfront.net (CloudFront)
9 X-Amz-Cf-Id: _y_e0gjS2U1RcJ8yknRPGjYB5coSSyeG1vkV9-IKaHGUUBs03-900A==
10 Connection: Keep-alive
```

UpdateFilter

Updates the filter specified by the filter name.

Request Syntax

```
1 POST https://<endpoint>/detector/{detectorId}/filter/<filter-name>
```

Body:

```
1    {
2      "description": "string",
3      "criteria":  [
4          "criterion": {
5              "<field>": {
6                  "gt": "integer",
7                  "gte": "integer",
8                  "lt": "integer",
9                  "lte": "integer",
10                 "eq": [
11                     "string"
12                 ],
13                 "neq": [
14                     "string"
15                 ]
16             }
17         }
18     ],
19     "action": "[NOOP|ARCHIVE]",
20     "rank": "integer"
21   }
```

Path Parameters

detectorID
The unique ID of the detector that specifies the GuardDuty service where you want to update a filter.
Type: String
Required: Yes

filterName
The name of the filter.
Type: String
Required: Yes

Request Parameters

The request accepts the following data in JSON format.

description
The description of the filter.
Type: String
Required: No

findingCriteria

Represents the criteria to be used in the filter for querying findings.

Type: FindingCriteria

Required: No

You can only use the following attributes to query findings:

[See the AWS documentation website for more details]

Gt

Represents the "greater than" condition to be applied to a single field when querying for findings.

Required: No

Gte

Represents the "greater than equal" condition to be applied to a single field when querying for findings.

Required: No

Lt

Represents the "less than" condition to be applied to a single field when querying for findings.

Required: No

Lte

Represents the "less than equal" condition to be applied to a single field when querying for findings.

Required: No

Eq

Represents the "equal to" condition to be applied to a single field when querying for findings.

Required: No

Neq

Represents the "not equal to" condition to be applied to a single field when querying for findings.

Required: No

action

Specifies the action that is to be applied to the findings that match the filter.

Type: Enum

Required: No

Valid values: NOOP | ARCHIVE

rank

Specifies the position of the filter in the list of current filters. Also specifies the order in which this filter is applied to the findings.

Type: Integer

Required: No

Constraints: Minimum value is 1 and maximum value is equal to the increment of the total number of current filters.

Response Syntax

```
1 {
2         "name": "string"
3 }
```

Response Elements

If the action is successful, the service sends back an HTTP 200 response.

name

The name of the filter.

Errors

If the action is not successful, the service sends back an HTTP error response code along with detailed error information.

InvalidInputException

The request is rejected. The required query or path parameters are not specified.

HTTP Status Code: 400

InvalidInputException

The request is rejected. One or more input parameters have invalid values.

HTTP Status Code: 400

InvalidInputException

The request is rejected. The parameter `detectorId` has an invalid value.

HTTP Status Code: 400

InvalidInputException

The request is rejected. The parameter `name` has an invalid value.

HTTP Status Code: 400

InvalidInputException

The request is rejected. The parameter `description` has an invalid value.

HTTP Status Code: 400

InvalidInputException

The request is rejected. The parameter `findingCriteria` has an invalid value.

HTTP Status Code: 400

InvalidInputException

The request is rejected. The parameter `action` has an invalid value.

HTTP Status Code: 400

InvalidInputException

The request is rejected. The parameter `rank` has an invalid value.

HTTP Status Code: 400

NoSuchEntityException

The request is rejected. The input `detectorId` is not owned by the current account.

HTTP Status Code: 400

AccessDeniedException

The request is rejected. The caller is not authorized to call this API.

HTTP Status Code: 400

NoSuchEntityException

The request is rejected. The input `name` is not owned by the current account.

HTTP Status Code: 400

InternalException

Internal server error.

HTTP Status Code: 500

Example

Sample Request

```
1 POST /detector/12abc34d567e8fa901bc2d34e56789f0 HTTP/1.1
2 Host: guardduty.us-west-2.amazonaws.com
3 Accept-Encoding: identity
4 Content-Length: 16
5 Authorization: AUTHPARAMS
6 X-Amz-Date: 20180123T231356Z
7 User-Agent: aws-cli/1.14.29 Python/2.7.9 Windows/8 botocore/1.8.33
8 {
9     "enable":true
10 }
```

Sample Response

```
1 HTTP/1.1 200 OK
2 Content-Type: application/json
3 Content-Length: 0
4 Date: Tue, 23 Jan 2018 23:13:57 GMT
5 x-amzn-RequestId: 16c23992-0093-11e8-a33d-67e86e7cc0b9
6 X-Amzn-Trace-Id: sampled=0;root=1-5a67c1b5-f8ce3625e119d47f2531e4ac
7 X-Cache: Miss from cloudfront
8 Via: 1.1 b7b35e3be0ac217c56fb0eb4da9b75bb.cloudfront.net (CloudFront)
9 X-Amz-Cf-Id: _y_e0gjS2U1RcJ8yknRPGjYB5coSSyeG1vkV9-IKaHGUUBs03-900A==
10 Connection: Keep-alive
```

UpdateFindingsFeedback

Marks specified Amazon GuardDuty findings as useful or not useful.

Request Syntax

```
1 POST https://<endpoint>/detector/{detectorId}/findings/feedback
```

Body:

```
1 {
2     "findingIds": [
3         "string"
4     ],
5     "feedback": "[USEFUL|NOT_USEFUL]",
6     "comments": "string"
7 }
```

Request Parameters

detectorId
The detector ID of the GuardDuty service whose findings you want to mark as useful or not useful.
Type: String

Request Parameters

The request accepts the following data in JSON format.

findingIds
The IDs of the findings that you want to mark as useful or not useful.
Type: Array of strings. Minimum number of 0 items. Maximum number of 50.
Required: Yes

feedback
Type: String
Required: Yes
Valid values: USEFUL | NOT_USEFUL

comments
Additional feedback about the GuardDuty findings.
Type: String
Required: No
Limits: maximum of 160 characters. Supported characters include only a-z, A-Z, 0-9, and single and double quotes.

Response Elements

If the action is successful, the service sends back an HTTP 200 response.

Errors

If the action is not successful, the service sends back an HTTP error response code along with detailed error information.

InvalidInputException

The request is rejected. The required query or path parameters are not specified.

HTTP Status Code: 400

InvalidInputException

The request is rejected. One or more input parameters have invalid values.

HTTP Status Code: 400

InvalidInputException

The request is rejected. An invalid or out-of-range value is specified as an input parameter.

HTTP Status Code: 400

InvalidInputException

The request is rejected. The parameter `detectorId` has an invalid value.

HTTP Status Code: 400

InvalidInputException

The request is rejected. The parameter comment has an invalid value.

HTTP Status Code: 400

InvalidInputException

The request is rejected. The number of requested finding IDs is out-of-bounds.

HTTP Status Code: 400

NoSuchEntityException

The request is rejected. The input `detectorId` is not owned by the current account.

HTTP Status Code: 400

InternalException

Internal server error.

HTTP Status Code: 500

Example

Sample Request

```
1 POST /detector/c6b0be64463ff852400d8ae5b2353866/findings/feedback HTTP/1.1
2 Host: guardduty.us-west-2.amazonaws.com
3 Accept-Encoding: identity
4 Content-Length: 78
5 Authorization: AUTHPARAMS
6 X-Amz-Date: 20180209T230429Z
7 User-Agent: aws-cli/1.14.29 Python/2.7.9 Windows/8 botocore/1.8.33
8 {
9    "findingIds":[
```

```
10        "9cb0be64df8ba1df249c45eb8a0bf584"
11    ],
12    "feedback":"NOT_USEFUL"
13 }
```

Sample Response

```
1 HTTP/1.1 200 OK
2 Content-Type: application/json
3 Content-Length: 0
4 Date: Fri, 09 Feb 2018 23:04:30 GMT
5 x-amzn-RequestId: 9599e105-0ded-11e8-a294-df0cbca23ced
6 X-Amzn-Trace-Id: sampled=0;root=1-5a7e28fe-885816710d8ec164f83ae38d
7 X-Cache: Miss from cloudfront
8 Via: 1.1 33cfbeb7154bbef1432b207659c6dac5.cloudfront.net (CloudFront)
9 X-Amz-Cf-Id: Z6_YLuTs4hTxC5OUgUUVwoqhEALPrE9HyelAd-6qxmRViJOOL6bjcA==
10 Connection: Keep-alive
```

UpdateIPSet

Updates the IPSet that is specified by the IPSet ID.

Important
Users from GuardDuty member accounts cannot run this API. Currently in GuardDuty, users from member accounts CANNOT upload and further manage IPSets. IPSets that are uploaded by the master account are imposed on GuardDuty functionality in its member accounts. For more information, see Managing AWS Accounts in Amazon GuardDuty.

Request Syntax

```
1 POST https://<endpoint>/detector/{detectorId}/ipset/{ipSetId}
```

Body:

```
1 {
2     "name": "string",
3     "location": "string",
4     "activate": "boolean"
5 }
```

Path Parameters

detectorId
The detector ID that specifies the GuardDuty service whose IPSet you want to update.
Type: String
Required: Yes

ipSetId
The unique ID that specifies the IPSet that you want to update.
Type: String
Required: Yes

Request Parameters

The request accepts the following data in JSON format.

name
The updated friendly name for the IPSet.
Type: String
Required: No

location
The updated URI of the file that contains the IPSet.
Type: String
Required: No

activate
Specifies whether the IPSet is active or not.
Type: Boolean
Required: No

Response Syntax

If the action is successful, the service sends back an HTTP 200 response.

Errors

If the action is not successful, the service sends back an HTTP error response code along with detailed error information.

InvalidInputException

The request is rejected. An invalid or out-of-range value is specified as an input parameter.

HTTP Status Code: 400

InvalidInputException

The request is rejected. The required query or path parameters are not specified.

HTTP Status Code: 400

InvalidInputException

The request is rejected. One or more input parameters have invalid values.

HTTP Status Code: 400

InvalidInputException

The request is rejected. The parameter `detectorId` has an invalid value.

HTTP Status Code: 400

InvalidInputException

The request is rejected. An invalid `ipSetId` is specified.

HTTP Status Code: 400

InvalidInputException

The request is rejected. Member accounts cannot manage IPSets or ThreatIntelSets.

HTTP Status Code: 400

NoSuchEntityException

The request is rejected. The input `detectorId` is not owned by the current account.

HTTP Status Code: 400

NoSuchEntityException

The request is rejected. An invalid `ipSetId` is specified.

HTTP Status Code: 400

AccessDeniedException

The request is rejected. The caller is not authorized to call this API.

HTTP Status Code: 400

NoSuchEntityException

The request is rejected. No role was found.

HTTP Status Code: 400

BadRequestException

The request is rejected. The service can't assume the service role.

HTTP Status Code: 400

AccessDeniedException

The request is rejected. You do not have the required `iam:PutRolePolicy` permission.

HTTP Status Code: 400

BadRequestException

The request is rejected. The specified service role is not a service role.

HTTP Status Code: 400

InternalException

Internal server error.

HTTP Status Code: 500

Example

Sample Request

```
1 POST /detector/12abc34d567e8fa901bc2d34e56789f0/ipset/0cb0141ab9fbde177613ab9436212e90 HTTP/1.1
2 Host: guardduty.us-west-2.amazonaws.com
3 Accept-Encoding: identity
4 Content-Length: 19
5 Authorization: AUTHPARAMS
6 X-Amz-Date: 20180124T002823Z
7 User-Agent: aws-cli/1.14.29 Python/2.7.9 Windows/8 botocore/1.8.33
8 {
9    "activate":false
10 }
```

Sample Response

```
1 HTTP/1.1 200 OK
2 Content-Type: application/json
3 Content-Length: 0
4 Date: Wed, 24 Jan 2018 00:28:25 GMT
5 x-amzn-RequestId: 7d04eb7e-009d-11e8-9150-9b7ab09573a9
6 X-Amzn-Trace-Id: sampled=0;root=1-5a67d328-1f5cd901719c010f77e58ee3
7 X-Cache: Miss from cloudfront
8 Via: 1.1 2d8af5cc5befc5d35bb54b4a5b6494c9.cloudfront.net (CloudFront)
9 X-Amz-Cf-Id: 9yHsYLUD63GBTsSwOGPBRRDtoU5m_Ncv9LAJ-EmknNTNxi9wzCOzew==
10 Connection: Keep-alive
```

UpdateThreatIntelSet

Updates the ThreatIntelSet that is specified by the ThreatIntelSet ID.

Important
Users from GuardDuty member accounts cannot run this API. Currently in GuardDuty, users from member accounts CANNOT upload and further manage ThreatIntelSets. ThreatIntelSets that are uploaded by the master account are imposed on GuardDuty functionality in its member accounts. For more information, see Managing AWS Accounts in Amazon GuardDuty.

Request Syntax

```
1 POST https://<endpoint>/detector/{detectorId}/threatintelset/{threatIntelSetId}
```

Body:

```
1 {
2     "name": "string",
3     "location": "string",
4     "activate": "boolean"
5 }
```

Path Parameters

detectorId
The detector ID that specifies the GuardDuty service whose ThreatIntelSet you want to update.
Type: String
Required: Yes

threatIntelSetId
The unique ID that specifies the ThreatIntelSet that you want to update.
Type: String
Required: Yes

Request Parameters

The request accepts the following data in JSON format.

name
The updated friendly name for the ThreatIntelSet.
Type: String
Required: No

location
The updated URI of the file that contains the ThreatIntelSet.
Type: String
Required: No

activate
Specifies whether the ThreateIntelSet is active or not.
Required: No
Type: Boolean

Response Syntax

If the action is successful, the service sends back an HTTP 200 response.

Errors

If the action is not successful, the service sends back an HTTP error response code along with detailed error information.

InvalidInputException

The request is rejected. An invalid or out-of-range value is specified as an input parameter.

HTTP Status Code: 400

InvalidInputException

The request is rejected. The required query or path parameters are not specified.

HTTP Status Code: 400

InvalidInputException

The request is rejected. One or more input parameters have invalid values.

HTTP Status Code: 400

InvalidInputException

The request is rejected. The parameter `detectorId` has an invalid value.

HTTP Status Code: 400

InvalidInputException

The request is rejected. An invalid `ipSetId` is specified.

HTTP Status Code: 400

InvalidInputException

The request is rejected. Member accounts cannot manage IPSets or ThreatIntelSets.

HTTP Status Code: 400

NoSuchEntityException

The request is rejected. The input `detectorId` is not owned by the current account.

HTTP Status Code: 400

NoSuchEntityException

The request is rejected. An invalid `ipSetId` is specified.

HTTP Status Code: 400

AccessDeniedException

The request is rejected. The caller is not authorized to call this API.

HTTP Status Code: 400

NoSuchEntityException

The request is rejected. No role was found.

HTTP Status Code: 400

BadRequestException

The request is rejected. The service can't assume the service role.

HTTP Status Code: 400

AccessDeniedException

The request is rejected. You do not have the required `iam:PutRolePolicy` permission.

HTTP Status Code: 400

BadRequestException

The request is rejected. The specified service role is not a service-linked role.

HTTP Status Code: 400

InternalException

Internal server error.

HTTP Status Code: 500

Example

Sample Request

```
1 POST /detector/12abc34d567e8fa901bc2d34e56789f0/threatintelset/8cb094db7082fd0db09479755d215dba
      HTTP/1.1
2 Host: guardduty.us-west-2.amazonaws.com
3 Accept-Encoding: identity
4 Content-Length: 19
5 Authorization: AUTHPARAMS
6 X-Amz-Date: 20180124T212506Z
7 User-Agent: aws-cli/1.14.29 Python/2.7.9 Windows/8 botocore/1.8.33
8 {
9    "activate":false
10 }
```

Sample Response

```
1 HTTP/1.1 200 OK
2 Content-Type: application/json
3 Content-Length: 0
4 Date: Wed, 24 Jan 2018 21:25:09 GMT
5 x-amzn-RequestId: 0d3e8284-014d-11e8-beb7-958380c0c8da
6 X-Amzn-Trace-Id: sampled=0;root=1-5a68f9b4-00718037918ec6f8abaacddd
7 X-Cache: Miss from cloudfront
8 Via: 1.1 7a06af51e583997d8673ab89482dd45a.cloudfront.net (CloudFront)
9 X-Amz-Cf-Id: 1YgXeOCWt1SC7nBaB2s8unBvIfhp45JRVJxXL3B-KHRWByGMCAyNRA==
10 Connection: Keep-alive
```

Document History for Amazon GuardDuty

Change	Description	Date
Added support for GuardDuty auto-archive rules	Customers can now build granular auto-archive rules for suppression of findings. For findings that match an auto-archive rule, GuardDuty automatically marks them as archived. This enables customers to further tune GuardDuty to keep only relevant findings in the current findings table. Learn more	May 4, 2018
GuardDuty is available in the EU (Paris) region	GuardDuty is now available in EU (Paris), allowing you to extend continuous security monitoring and threat detection to AWS' newest EU region. Learn more	March 29, 2018
Creating GuardDuty master and member accounts through AWS CloudFormation is now supported.	For more information, see AWS::GuardDuty::Master and AWS::GuardDuty::Member.	March 6, 2018
Added nine new CloudTrail-based anomaly detections.	These new finding types are automatically enabled in GuardDuty in all supported regions. Learn more	February 28, 2018
Added three new threat intelligence detections (finding types).	These new finding types are automatically enabled in GuardDuty in all supported regions. Learn more	February 5, 2018
Limit increase for GuardDuty member accounts.	With this release, you can have up to 1000 GuardDuty member accounts added per AWS account (GuardDuty master account). Learn more	January 25, 2018
Changes in upload and further management of trusted IP lists and threat lists for GuardDuty master and member accounts.	With this release, Users from master GuardDuty accounts can upload and manage trusted IP lists and threat lists. Users from member GuardDuty accounts CANNOT upload and manage lists. Trusted IP lists and threat lists that are uploaded by the master account are imposed on GuardDuty functionality in its member accounts. Learn more	January 25, 2018

The following table describes important changes in each release of the *GuardDuty* User Guide.

Earlier updates

Change	Description	Date
Initial publication	Initial publication of the Amazon GuardDuty User Guide.	November 28, 2017

AWS Glossary

For the latest AWS terminology, see the AWS Glossary in the *AWS General Reference.*